SITE, SIGHT, INSIGHT

Penn Studies in Landscape Architecture

John Dixon Hunt, Series Editor

This series is dedicated to the study and promotion of a wide variety of approaches to landscape architecture, with special emphasis on connections between theory and practice. It includes monographs on key topics in history and theory, descriptions of projects by both established and rising designers, translations of major foreign-language texts, anthologies of theoretical and historical writings on classic issues, and critical writing by members of the profession of landscape architecture.

The series was the recipient of the Award of Honor in Communications from the American Society of Landscape Architects, 2006.

SITE, SIGHT, INSIGHT

ESSAYS *on* LANDSCAPE ARCHITECTURE

John Dixon Hunt

Foreword by
 Peter Walker and Jane Brown Gillette

PENN University of Pennsylvania Press *Philadelphia*

Published by
University of Pennsylvania Press
Philadelphia, Pennsylvania 19104-4112
www.upenn.edu/pennpress

Printed in the United States of America on acid-free paper
10 9 8 7 6 5 4 3 2 1

Library of Congress Cataloging-in-Publication Data

Names: Hunt, John Dixon, author. | Walker, Peter, writer of preface. |
    Gillette, Jane Brown, writer of preface. | Hunt, John Dixon. Lie of the
    land. Container of (work):
Title: Site, sight, insight : essays on landscape architecture / John Dixon
    Hunt ; foreword by Peter Walker and Jane Brown Gillette.
Other titles: Penn studies in landscape architecture.
Description: Philadelphia : University of Pennsylvania Press, [2016] |
    Series: Penn studies in landscape architecture | Collection of essays;
    some are revisions of previously published texts. | Includes
    bibliographical references and index.
Identifiers: LCCN 2015039600 | ISBN 9780812248005 (alk. paper)
Subjects: LCSH: Landscape architecture. | Gardens—Philosophy.
Classification: LCC SB469.37 .H865 2016 | DDC 712—dc23
LC record available at http://lccn.loc.gov/2015039600

IN MEMORIAM
Sydney and Marjorie Hunt
&
Frank and Alice Dixon

Contents

Contents

Foreword

Peter Walker and Jane Brown Gillette

WE SHARE WITH John Dixon Hunt a love of gardens, current and historic, in perfection and decay. We like to experience them in various seasons and times of day, to contemplate and enjoy and assess their artistry. We also like to discuss and criticize them and read and write about them. We do this, of course, from quite different points of view. John loves to be in gardens, as do many of us who design and build them. But John brings to his visits a critical, informed eye that is founded on his background in literary and art history, and it is this difference that makes him so valuable to the field of landscape architecture.

In one essay in this collection John describes a pivotal moment in his career. At an IFLA conference in 1992 he expressed the thought that he might become a landscape architect, and Pete, presumably, shouted "from the rear of the hall . . . (something like) 'No, no; go on doing what you do.'" Pete Walker must admit that he has no memory of making this statement, but John's book of essays proves that the advice, whether his or not, was wise. Landscape architects need garden historians.

Over the years, the field of landscape architecture has enjoyed little critical discourse compared to architecture, planning, and the other visual and environmental arts. For the most part we have focused our critical energies on either ecological or planning issues with little attention to the design and art and significance of gardens and other cultural landscapes—which, as is the case with any other craft, can only be lifted to their highest possibilities through intelligent criticism and a thorough understanding of their historical backgrounds. Unfortunately landscape education today is particularly weak in design criticism and history, as opposed to what we call theory, a variety of discourse seldom put in its historical context and thus frequently serving, at best, as an offshoot of advertising even as its academic voice grows louder. Meanwhile most landscape architecture students are lucky to receive a single history course, which is rarely taught by a trained historian. Occasionally, this course is augmented by a random architectural or art history course with little or no defined relationship to the practice and history of landscape architecture.

When we visit a fine garden or designed landscape, we experience a unique work of great complexity in purpose, which has been executed over a number of years—a work that, occasionally, achieves beauty. Such landscapes contain built structure, living plants, and water, all with the ability to express, exploit, and sustain the changes and impacts of the natural elements through time. A creation of such complexity is all too frequently invisible to the general public (and to many professionals) without an explanation derived from a critical discourse that relates it to other elements of cultural endeavor, some genre related, some historical. This discourse can certainly include and be enriched by designers, but we are not trained historians or critical theoreticians and frequently lack the wide-reaching literacy that informs such professions.

The importance of this literacy can be evidenced by many examples in *Site, Sight, Insight,* but one must suffice. Throughout the essays John gives voice to a pervasive concern with our intellectual and aesthetic understanding of gardens: How do they affect us emotionally? Do they have "meaning"? What does "meaning" mean? Couldn't "meaning" more accurately be called "significance"? In these essays, initially published in a wide range of venues, John is particularly adept at discussing the issue of significance as it relates to subjects like follies, ekphrasis, bridges, and memory, as well as site-specific expressions at Stourhead and a host of other gardens. He states the problem and suggests a solution, and he shows a profound humanity in his willingness to end his argument in inconclusiveness, in possibility, in an indeterminate state so difficult for most of us to accept. John points to a solution to the problem of "meaning" in his essay on Stourhead: maybe we understand the garden in a way that corresponds to the eighteenth-century belief in "association," notably put forth in the philosophy of John Locke. According to this theory of human psychology, a garden—rather than the exposition of a single "meaning"—inspires a variety of associations from each of us when we visit its confines. In later essays John also points to the problem of free association: if everything in a garden can mean anything, doesn't significance of any importance evaporate? In the face of this problem, John expresses a desire for a core of learning that would shape our associations, learning that can only come from the study of form and history and critical rhetoric, a sort of common understanding and perception shaped by sophisticated perception and knowledge. In other words, we would abandon the exposition of one "meaning" in a landscape for a significance that comes about from a flow of informed associations. Such an approach to significance would require a careful examination of the physical landscape and much historical education, not only for landscape architects but for the public in general. Indeed, such an approach might even call for undergraduate courses in landscape history and a recognition that, like literary history and art history and social history, the history of gardens is a necessary part of the liberal arts education.

This one example of John's ability to state a problem and find a solution shows why we both have such a deep appreciation of his broad and scholarly point of view. We continue to profit from his energetic work in teaching, writing, and expanding publications pertinent to our understanding and practice of design.

Preface

THIS COLLECTION BRINGS together some of my recent writings on landscape architecture. Its common theme is a focus on sites, on how we see them and on what we derive from that looking. They reprise other sites about which I have written elsewhere, and they also allow some cross-references, even some overlaps, between the essays, since I have been pursuing these themes for some time, and certain topics recur on different occasions for different purposes. So I return frequently to a cluster of key sites and writings, upon which I have based much of my thinking about garden making and its role in landscape architecture: the gardens of Rousham in Oxfordshire, Thomas Whately's *Observations on Modern Gardening* (1770), William Gilpin's dialogue on Stowe (1747), Alexander Pope's meditation on genius loci, and sites like the Désert de Retz, Paolo Burgi's Cardada, and several designs by Bernard Lassus and Ian Hamilton Finlay.

Six of these essays are published here for the first time, the remainder, most of which originally appeared in publications where those interested in landscape architecture are less likely to look, have all been significantly revised. The one piece which I have barely changed, but to which I have now added some images, is the essay on the meaning of Stourhead that was first published in the journal that I have edited since its inception in 1981. I like to think it is one of the more useful pieces I have written, as it tackles the tricky issue of how we today read historical gardens, a topic that I feel still needs to be aired, and it endorses what I had taken up two years earlier in *The Afterlife of Gardens* (2004). Otherwise, the essays are versions of talks given in Portugal, Paris, Versailles, and London, and in graduate seminars at Penn that circle around the topics of site, sight, and insight; that on "ARCH" borrows a small segment of a piece that I wrote for the festschrift for Michael Seiler, *Wege zum Garten* (Potsdam, 2004). I have not attempted to "flatten" out these different talks and essays, but leave each to address a different audience. Finally, I have added a postscript to answer the question I am often asked—why did you move from literature to landscape? I never have enough time to explain why, or what the benefits of such an academic transition might be, so I offer it here.

Warm thanks for contributing their Foreword are due to Peter Walker, a distinguished landscape architect, and Jane Brown Gillette, a wonderful writer, whose path crossed mine when I was teaching English at Vassar College years ago.

I acknowledge good advice, as always, from Michael Leslie, David Leatherbarrow, and Edward Harwood on some of these collected essays, as well as comments from an anonymous reader.

The *Lie* of the Land

*This essay goes beyond issues of site, sight, and insight to explore
the sleight of hand by which landscape architects reformulate
the topography of the places they make.*

It is all too easy to imagine perfectly clean environments that are not
attractive at all. By contrast, it is quite possible to appreciate landscapes
that, from the environmental point of view, leave a lot to be desired.
—Bernard Lassus

THE LIE OF the land is topography, how it lies across the land—including
the base materials of its fundamental geology and what has happened to the
land in the course of different climatic and cultural responses to it, including its historical associations. But it is also that designed land "lies" or tells
untruths about itself, by virtue of whatever landscape architects do to it—
grading, introduction of new materials (plants, buildings), and the invention
of historical associations that do not belong there.[1] My argument is that all
designed landscapes can do both: they utilize the given materials, tell truth,
and yet also, through falsehood or untruths, enlarge or animate the site where
they intervene. (And it should be noted that all cultures at various times perform that intervention differently—as I can suggest later.) My further argument is that all landscape design needs to declare itself: a design that is not
noticed is not a good design. The frequent complaint about Capability Brown
is that you couldn't see any difference between his work and "common fields,"

and those folk who think Central Park is just "nature" are likely to miss the point of good design. Designs *are* art, and need to be acknowledged as such— exactly what lies behind one of Bernard Lassus's remarks on what we might expect from landscape designs.[2] We do not read a novel or see a movie without registering that it is a fiction or an invented narrative. And I see no reason why landscape architecture should try to get under that radar.

There have been moments clearly when the need to acknowledge topography is primary: when Alphonse Alphand in the later nineteenth century wrote his historical account of garden history to introduce *Les promenades de Paris*, he was assuming that a designer must consider a site undisturbed by human intervention; so he insisted that the designer needed to study the site, since the place, its geology and its topography, had a historical hinterland. "Le relief du terrain est la première chose à étudier . . . surtout quand le terrain est nu. Elle doit indiquer . . . le movement des vallées, determiner le lit des rivières, l'emplacement des pièces d'eau, c'est-à-dire les parties capitales du plan" (the lie of the land is the first thing to study . . . above all when the terrain is bare; notably indicating the shape of valleys, determining the beds of river, water features, which is to say the central elements of the [proposed] plan). Alphand continued by listing the natural accidents of the site, which might determine the principal aspects of the new design; however, he also noted that reworking the earth "pour composer un relief de fantaisie est un mauvais système qui aboutit, presque toujours, à une deception, après d'énormes dépenses" (to compose a plan out of one's fancy is a bad system that will almost always deceive and incur enormous expenses: p. xlix). He may well have been thinking of an earlier landscape architect, Jean-Marie Morel, also trained as an engineer, like himself, at the École des Ponts et Chaussées. Morel, the first designer to be called a landscape architect ("architecte-paysagiste"), was an expert at "identifying, interpreting, and recording" the components of landscape,[3] and his analysis of landforms was based upon his engineer's instinct and his knowledge of the processes of the natural world. But neither Alphand nor Morel produced anything that was not clearly and visibly an artifact; not fantasies, but fictions.

All insertions into the material world by landscape architects work in two ways: either they simply take the land that is given to them—its geology, its topography, what has happened to it in the course of different cultural responses to it, and thus also its historical associations; or they rework what is given, ignoring some of things they find there in order to promote their own imaginative response. Much more likely, there will be a mix of these two modes. That is what Alexander Pope argued in the 1730s when he wrote his "Epistle to Burlington" and clearly showed that genius loci is both the very materials of the site and what a designer (a different genius) makes of its materials by intervening on the site.

These insertions or reworkings derive from, or rely upon, a whole world of human experience. Not all of which, these days at least, comes from the land itself (I am not talking about Paleolithic gardeners who probably knew little about anything except the earth beneath their feet). Today, insertions by landscape architects come rather from a conspectus of ideas about land acquired from the need to respond to how people like to behave, from social and legal administration, but also from other unlegislated ideas—from painting, writing, and even other, earlier landscapes (some of which may be designed, others not). This last, both literally and metaphorically, may be called "travel": it was J. B. Jackson who argued that "tourism is a desire to know more about the world in order to know more about ourselves."[4] He meant actual travel, seeing more of the world; but it also meant what we might call "armchair traveling" of various sorts (not just reading guidebooks). Indeed, the word and the concept of "land" itself morphed, by the early eighteenth century, from the simple materials of the earth into the word "landscape," a Germanic-Dutch word that meant either a political unit of administration (that is, knowing how the world functioned) or what a Dutch or Flemish painter would see in the land and depict.

One of the useful analogies used recently by landscape critics is that of the palimpsest, the various layers on a site that are there already or can be installed there by the designer. Our response to sites has therefore to be palimpsestial.[5] And palimpsests connect us also to the "lie" or possible untruths that can be entertained; for both the literal palimpsest or parchment, on which different texts have been inscribed, and the palimpsest that the French critic Gérard Genette discusses in his book *Palimpsests: Literature in the Second Degree*, where any text may extend itself into a myriad of paratexts that gloss or implicitly comment upon it, are a complex tissue of truths and not always compatible.

Writers who use or invoke palimpsests are consciously narrative beings, and our narratives are derived from a world of contacts—things we know directly, or things we collect indirectly from "travel." Some of these stories may be true, some may be wonderful fabrications, often manipulated deliberately or because memory plays tricks with us. And all of these involve "references" or allusions to the palimpsest of our lives. That said, no landscape architecture that I know exists independently of what humans know or want for themselves in the world; we all have memories and knowledge, and these are things that have come to us from a variety of places we know and from ideas that circulate for us—in movies, texts, paintings, and so on. Thus I want to insist that landscape too has contexts beyond the immediate physical materials of a site; these days we rarely stay in the same place all our lives, and even if we are born and live wholly in one place and never go elsewhere, we will undoubtedly know that place hugely and intimately from a careful understanding of what goes on there and from what people know of elsewhere. But generally we range and are curious while doing so.

Now here we must confront the issue of what contexts *are* apt, appropriate, or socially acceptable when we make landscapes, for obviously there will be contexts that we do not want drawn into the world of landscape architecture: we do not, for example, tolerate cruelty, ugliness, or chemical weapons. We don't make deliberately ugly places (true, these days we all have different notions of the ugly). But then every culture has different ideas about these things—which makes (for me) a nonsense of thinking that a landscape architect can work just anywhere. Nor, of course, can we include everything in any one design—it must simplify, must edit the world of our contexts. So contexts outside a site and contexts inside a site are the stuff that shapes design.

Let me postpone for a while elaborating on these theoretical propositions and look briefly at six pieces of landscape architecture from different periods of its history. In each, I want (i) to show how the landscaper responds to the land itself at the point when he (it was in those eras always a "he," I'm afraid) gets to intervene in it, and (ii) to suggest that the designer of the site, while he or she may use its geology, its topography, or its plant materials, more largely depends upon ideas from outside the site; these ideas change or reenvisage what the site holds by involving its visitors in responding to the new place. Hence my motto or caption for all this approach, as announced in the title of this book, is Site—Sight—Insight.[6] By site I mean the place for which a design is intended; by sight I mean how people look at it in its unmediated state, and afterward how visitors see it; by insight I mean how both designers and the site's users, or sometimes (alas) simply "consumers," respond to its ideas and feelings, what could be termed an "ambient" landscape.[7] Each of these sites is

1. Villa Lante, Bagnaia.
Photograph by Emily T. Cooperman.

informed by the given terrain, by what its landscapers or engineers can do to it, and by whatever ideas they or their clients expect of their work. So what informs these sites is a mixture, even a dialogue between, physical facts and materials and what the French call *mentalité,* sometimes very local, sometimes very wide ranging.

The site of the sixteenth-century Villa Lante, near Viterbo in Italy, is on a hillside, with water gathered in the hills behind it and captured in a reservoir to be used for the hydraulic effects within the garden (Figure 1). The hillside affords cool breezes, and the water refreshes, during the summer months. The engineering and hydrology create both a series of terraces and a succession of wonderful fountains as the water descends through the gardens, and these are graced with statues, a dining table, fountains, and a pair of little casinos decorated with images of other villas. We have therefore a site that is both natural—the water, the slope, the descending waters, and what the designers have achieved for it—but also peopled with an anthology of classical, biblical, and local references. The garden itself is juxtaposed to an adjacent hunting park as well as the wilder Apennines behind: thus we see at a glance how the garden itself arises out of, literally from, the topography, and how different treatments of that land have produced different ratios of control between the terraces and fountains, the river gods and Pegasus, on the one hand, and the more relaxed parkland, on the other, though that is also furnished with fountains among its pathways. Both garden and park are also registered as being in the middle, between the mountains above and the town below it, into which the waters flow.

The garden of Vaux-le-Vicomte, designed by André Le Nôtre, is composed of two slopes that meet at a canalized river that flows through the valley. Terraces descend from the chateau itself and on the far side of the canal rise into forests for hunting (Figure 2). But the river was canalized as it entered the grounds and recovers its river-ness as it leaves it—thus abstracting, formalizing the river so that its significance could be appreciated, or giving to natural features a sense of their forms. The garden is then marked with varied classical imagery, river gods in niches fronting the canal and a huge statue of Hercules set against the forest and looking down upon the gardens (recalling one of his mythical labors when he stole the golden apples from the Garden of the Hesperides).

Rousham in Oxfordshire also has a river, but in its path it has simply eroded the hillside as it wanders across the water meadows on the way to Oxford (Figure 3). The gardens that descend to that river occupy an irregular shape of land, into which two landscapers, Charles Bridgeman in the 1720s and then in 1739 William Kent, worked to enhance the site with statues, a temple and a pyramid, seats, a series of grottoes that descend the Vale of Venus where the goddess presides, theaters (a green theater-like stage by Bridgeman, later naturalized by Kent), and a wonderful single line of arcades that Kent borrowed from the temple of Fortune at Palestrina (a Genette-like palimpsest gesture). Kent especially plays with the Oxfordshire locality, alluding to Italy

2. The landscape of Vaux-le-Vicomte below the statue of Hercules at the edge of the forest. Photograph by Emily T. Cooperman.

and yet slyly registering how much must be changed in the particular topography and culture of England.

When Beth Meyer analyzed Brooklyn's Prospect Park[8] she saw that Olmsted and Vaux were right to expand the area of the proposed parkland to include three different geologies (Figure 4); in other words, they were relying on their knowledge of the geology there to enable them, by utilizing different topographies, to create a parkland that promoted a series of different experiences in the long meadow, the sublime dell, and the lake.

The Park of Buttes Chaumont (Figure 5), created by Alphand when Haussmann cleaned up Paris in the 1860s, took over a quarry, a rubbish dump, and a site where malefactors were displayed and turned the topography into a quite stunning site by celebrating what was new—the railways that ran through it, a modern bridge designed by Eiffel—and by enhancing the quarry remains with concrete reformations of its walls and on the edges of the new lake, making stalactites in a cavern and in the park, steps and railings also fashioned out of concrete to look like wood.

The modern Jardin de la Noria in Provence was designed by Eric Ossart and Arnaud Maurières, authors of *Jardiniers de Paradis* (2000). The site is a

3. The river at Rousham seen from the terrace beside the Praeneste Arcade. Photograph by the author.

former farm or *mas*, with plentiful water and the usual orchard and *potager*, but is now the new habitation of people moved down from Paris permanently, so it also now contains a swimming pool. What gives its name to the garden is the chance to privilege an ancient Arabic mechanism known as a *noria* (Figure 6) to draw water from the earth (this part of Provence is well fed by water), a device still found in parts of the Middle East and North Africa. The designers also referenced the Islamic Generalife in Spain with a long pool, and with a series of modern pots, seats, and chairs (the locality is named after a former

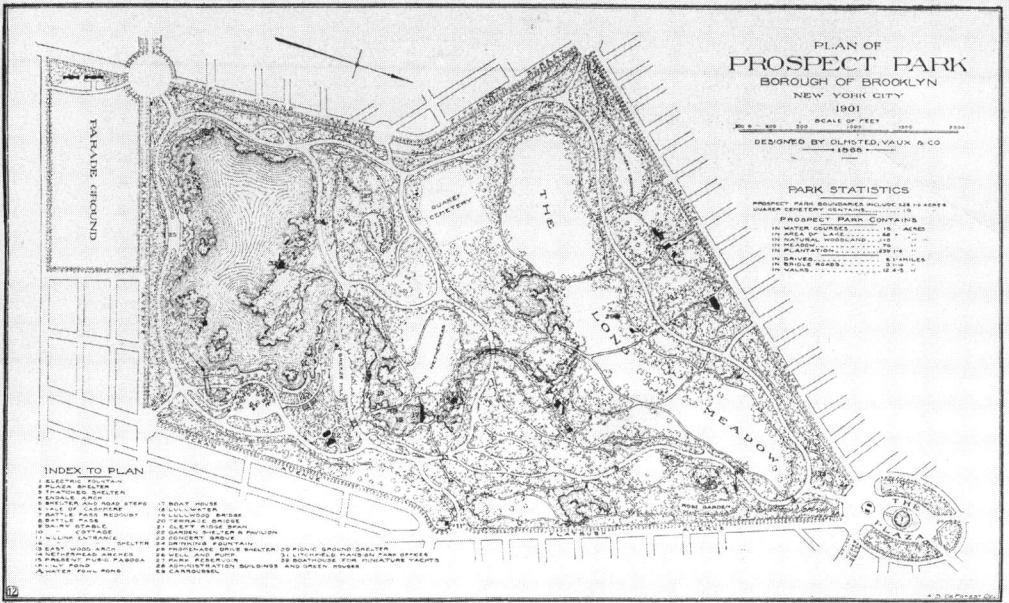

4. A map of the topography and design of Prospect Park, 1888. Private collection.

poterie, or ceramic works). These gestures to ancient hydrology, to Islamic gardens, and to modern garden forms are a Genette-like palimpsest that responds both to the site and to what the young designers brought to it from their Mediterranean observation of ancient gardens and their sense of local culture.

THE PHRASE "*lie* of the land" contains, then, two things. Both the sense of how the land performs itself, its texture, its material effects, its ups and downs, that is, what was there before anything happened through the work of landscape architecture (water most notably, climate, endemic plant species), but including probably everything that culture has done to it over the years (farming, trash dumps, hangings). Less obviously, the phrase means how the land is lying, telling falsehoods, faking something that was not there before but is there now, and that includes, of course, all sorts of cultural interventions on the land by the landscape architect—the recourse to allusion (classical deities, mythology), to knowledge of history (what happened there—trash

9

dumps or hangings), to his expertise in geology, and what he knows in the world (Mediterranean garden culture, its agriculture).

Now all art manages a glorious deceit; as Touchstone in *As You Like It* argues, "The truest poetry is the most feigning": art invents, or feigns, in order to persuade and entertain, and it does both by drawing on the *poet's* knowledge and imagination, which he then shares with us.[9] And this is true for landscape architecture. All art equally depends on our acceptance of its truthfulness, and this can change culturally from place to place and from age to age. A bad picture, a bad novel, a bad movie fails because people do not respond positively to it, perhaps because the invention is unconvincing or it meets an audience not yet prepared for it (now, of course, sometimes a great work—there are many—doesn't succeed at first and takes time to win people over; and equally, some works that strike an immediate chord later lose their appeal).

But I insist upon the combination of persuasion and entertainment in all great landscape architecture: if a place is not pleasant, congenial, useful (that is, with good amenities to suit the site where it is established), it will not please and entertain. But it will also need to persuade its users of something beyond

5. Engraved view of the Parc des Buttes Chaumont, Paris, c. 1860s.

6. The *noria* in the Jardin de la Noria, Provence.
Photograph by Emily T. Cooperman.

what is there; they may be able to "look" (that is, employ sight), but must be encouraged also to "see" (employ insight).

Let me give you another example, now from the work of Paolo Bürgi, presented as a contribution to the book *Field Studies* (Figure 7).[10] Called to respond to an unappetizing and moribund agricultural land and the threats of encroaching new houses, whose inhabitants disdained the nearby fields, what he did was to make the new suburban neighbors look and *see* the agricultural land anew: a series of inventive and very visible managements of the fields by plowing and sowing the corn with bands of colored flowers made the neighborhood look and see the topography better, while the farmer, who happily cooperated with the new working of the land, found a new relish for his fields.

Landscape architecture needs to be *seen as* (registered as) landscape architecture; there is no point in doing something if you don't notice it. And even in the simplest and most pragmatic ways bits and pieces of landscape architecture mean more than the item itself: athletic fields speak of health and fitness; parks provide opportunities for solitude, seats, and shade, solicit meditation and thoughtfulness; viewsheds ask for visitors to imagine what they see but cannot reach at that moment; other places clearly allow people to socialize, and that also implies much more than what the specific place offers. And that is where, I think, elements of landscape architecture, that are not endemic or

7. Paolo Bürgi, an image of the proposed manipulation of agricultural land. Reproduced with permission of the designer.

local to the site, can still manage to fuel people's imaginations. All the sites that I looked at are bigger, "larger" and more capacious, than the land itself, even after designers have worked to make it what we see.

Denis Cosgrove wrote that landscape was a way of seeing the world, and he meant cultural but nondesigned landscapes.[11] So I'd like to end by invoking both a photographer, actually not his work but what he wrote about it, and one more contemporary designed landscape. Robert Adams was a landscape photographer, influenced by the photography of Timothy O'Sullivan and William Henry Jackson, who first gained prominence through his involvement in the New Topographics movement.[12] In an essay entitled "Truth and Landscape," Adams discusses three "verities" of landscape photographs: geography, autobiography, and metaphor. As a photographer, he wants to understand the geography; he also wants his photographs to be "autobiographical." Now, I must insist that I do not think landscape architects can be autobiographical in the way that a photographer can be, so what I draw from Adams is that the photograph and thus the landscape has to respond personally to what he

8. Michael van Valkenburgh, Tear Drop Park, lower Manhattan. Photograph by Emily T. Cooperman.

sees (the geography), he has to make it his own, coherent within itself and not solely solipsist and overly personal. But finally, which is where I want to go, Adams asked for metaphor—this too I need to gloss as both something on the site and something that speaks metaphorically of other things not there.

Here Michael van Valkenburgh's Tear Drop Park in lower Manhattan (Figure 8) is illuminating: the site itself "lies"—for the area is formed by ground fill from the construction of the twin towers; then the small space between the new apartments is made "bigger" by what the designer puts it in, especially by the sheer invention of those bluestone walls, which echo (Genette-like) the materials and cuts of New York State thruways. Fabricated at full scale off site

13

and then reassembled in Tear Drop Park, they make the design at once meta-phorical, highly personal, and attentive to the place where it is. The ice that forms in the winter months augments the true poetry of its feigning.

The "lie" of the land, then, is both what the topography offers to us and the designer, and how the designer can use how the land lies for his own purposes and to appeal to the imaginations of those who visit that site in the future. Hence, there may be falsehoods or imaginative reinventions of it: therefore a feigned truth, which may be the truest poetry.

Chapter 2

Near and Far, and the Spaces in Between

> *Negotiating spaces in landscape architecture for a modern*
> *picturesque means finding a way of entering into and*
> *responding to the sites of designed landscapes by accepting the*
> *totality of a site and not just focusing on its discussable items;*
> *thus, the role of walking as well as seeing.*

IT WAS GENERALLY assumed in Western painting, which supposedly influenced landscape architecture, that the artist should think of his subject in the triadic terms of foreground, middle ground, and distance. A typical piece of advice from the French critic the Abbé Laugier in 1753 argued that gardeners should use this form of painting, where both distance and close-up, and the places in between, are essential. An exhibition at the Landesmuseum in Hanover, Germany, in 2011 with the title "Nah und Fern" ("Near and Far"),[1] was, on the face of it, a familiar exhibition of landscape images, well worth considering in their own right for the perspectival obligations of landscape painters and their viewers. But the "injunction," so to speak, of the exhibition's title encouraged one to look anew at these paintings.

In two respects it held implications for today's landscape architects. First, modernist paintings have not followed that triadic obligation: with their emphasis upon the materials and the ontology of the painting itself, with no concern for narrative or the need for perspective, paintings have tended to eliminate representations of a graded landscape from foreground into the distance; they would simply present a flat surface, on which the pigments and colors were laid down, with no indication of depth.[2] A perfect instance of this modernist attitude can be seen in a painting by the Frenchman Bernard Lassus, who first trained as a painter in the atelier of Ferdinand Léger before turning landscape architect (Figure 9).[3]

Second, this modernist attention to the format and significance of modernist paintings calls into question the significance of the picturesque as both a mode of design and a way of seeing landscape. It is generally acknowledged as a tired and crippling model for landscape design, as many landscape architects are quick to point out:

> Conventions of landscape practice and representation are thick with
> the sediment of habit and tradition. Often cited as a force behind those
> conventions is the early eighteenth-century English garden, the harbinger of
> the picturesque landscape. One particular understanding of the picturesque
> relates to the practice of comparing landscape scenes to, and composing them
> from, landscape paintings. Seeing landscape as a three-dimensional work that
> mimics a two-dimensional image sets up the stubbornly pervasive techniques
> and attitudes that currently define and delimit landscape's—and nature's—
> pictorialization.[4]

While one may pass over the historical misinformation here, what is interesting in such a comment is that it ignores how contemporary thinking about landscape, while still relying on the picturesque, has occasionally radically reformulated it: thus, it is a question, *not* of composing landscapes as if they were paintings, but of exploring three-dimensional landscapes (actually four-dimensional landscapes, if we allow the time taken to visit them and the time through which they have lived). This fresh concept is precisely what we can grasp at the moment when a painter like Lassus went on to achieve great success as a landscape architect. He perceived that—as a landscape designer, as opposed to being a painter—he was obliged to perceive and realize landscapes as having a similar triadic format—foreground, middle ground, and distance, but now understood in a different way.

IN THIS, Lassus may be said to be in the French tradition that began arguably with Denis Diderot's *Essai sur la peinture* and his writings on the Salon paintings of the 1760s, 1770s, and 1781. Diderot sought to lead viewers of contemporary paintings *into* the spaces of their imagined surface, as if it

9. Bernard Lassus, *Echelle Visuelle, Echelle Tactile*, 1956. Courtesy of the artist.

were a real landscape into which one could indeed penetrate,[5] and in which we could therefore respond to both the foreground and the background, and review the middle distance by walking through its intermediate spaces; these viewers/*promeneurs* could explore the ("imagined") places in between what the artist had depicted as being close to them and what was implied as being far away in the painting. This in its turn allowed space for rhetorical commentary on those intervening elements, even if they were without specific or significant incidents. In a famous account of paintings by Claude-Joseph Vernet in 1767, Diderot imagines a promenade invented "pour rompre l'ennui et la monotonie des descriptions" (to break the boredom and monotony of [mere] descriptions [of paintings]).[6] This is not the place to pursue Diderot's "excursions," since they have been well published and commented upon by scholars in both the republished writings edited by Jacques Chouillet and in the massive catalogue of 1984, *Diderot et l'art de Boucher à David*. But what is crucial is to realize that Diderot's response to painting landscapes transformed how paintings *and* landscapes could be encountered, how they were painted, and—above all—how they attained an afterlife for those who viewed them: no longer were paintings the object of bored and monotonous descriptions, instead they elicited an animated and detailed response to everything within their (imagined) scenery, as if the viewer were actually wandering in them. Doubtless, the first-hand experience that Diderot had learnt by exploring new mid-century landscape designs in France was translated into his pictorial analysis.

I would suggest that Diderot's prototypical excursions are exactly equivalent to how modernist landscape architects can and should respond to their own design work, and how we may in our turn understand them (breaking, perhaps, with our own sense of boredom and monotony with "mere" pictorialism). Indeed, the "modernity" of Diderot's criticism has been explored by Régis Michel in the catalogue already cited (pp. 110–21); but it needs now to be extended into the world of landscape making and response.

Here the work of Bernard Lassus is extremely useful. As a landscape architect Lassus still needed the triadic formulas of conventional painting. But now not as imaginary, even if flat, surfaces, but—like Diderot—as real sites where nearness, distance, and what lay between them can be explored and where we must negotiate them mentally as well as physically. This attention to the spaces in between the near and the far raised other issues for landscape architecture, which Lassus himself explored within the concept of modernism: specifically, the differences between what can be touched or what can only be seen in an actual landscape, on the one hand, and, on the other, the fact that being able to move through a landscape meant that one could eventually touch what before had only been seen. (For there is also a temporal or historical register of what is in front of us and what is yet to be discovered or seen in the past or the future.) Landscape was, in short, a territory in which the near and the far could be explored and therefore were interchangeable, thereby opening up the spaces in between for reflection. And while this theme may originate in the painterly mind, it has its reverberations beyond the practical responses of a painter.

Others have explored this dialogue in their own disciples: Claude Lévi-Strauss explained it in *De près et de loin*, a book of conversations with Didier Eribon (Paris: Odile Jacob, 1988). Here the near and far of his title are the actual intersections of the near—present-day Paris—with the faraway experiences of this famous anthropologist, and also point to the way in which, pondering his career, Lévi-Strauss reflects in the present on how his earlier experiences and publications have to be narrated and refigured at the immediate moment of their conversations. That the father and two uncles of Lévi-Strauss were also painters suggest how much his reminiscences might be a consequence of their artistic attention to the problematic of foreground and background and how it essentially functions as the structure and leitmotif of his own autobiographical reflections.

An artist, and in his case a distinguished landscape architect, like Laurie Olin also makes much of how he sees and draws the near and far, literally and phenomenologically. In his book *Across the Open Field* his drawings often show both close-up and distant views that imply both a careful consideration of the tactile and the visual and their potent exchange in how we respond to these landscapes (Figure 10). Olin manages with his bifocal images to give a different sense of depth of field in these landscapes; if we look first at the close-up images of plants—higher up the page, closer to us—and then the distant landscape at the bottom of the page, we transpose our knowledge of the first into what we imagine we'd find in the latter.

Ian Hamilton Finlay, too, in a commentary on his work by Yves Abrioux, sees potential in "the interplay between proximity and distance."[7] Using early written stories by Finlay, Abrioux sees strange conjunctions/disjunctions in phenomena both visionary and imagined. In the garden that he and his wife, Sue, established at Little Sparta in Scotland, Finlay played with what was there and what was either far away or not even visible: he invoked the sea in this inland garden; in both a poem and later with his construction of walls to celebrate "LITTLE FIELDS LONG HORIZONS," he asked us to see and think about this juxtaposition. The concrete poem plays with the words "fir" and "far," and Finlay repeats the word "fir" to give the illusion of looking down a tapering woodland grove at the "end" of which we see the single word "far." For this Abrioux cites a useful aperçu by Walter Benjamin—"the unique phenomenon of distance, however close it may be."

ALL THIS connects with Lassus, whose introduction to Finlay's *Selected Ponds* enunciates the theme of what he terms the "immeasurable," an ambiguous play with near and far.[8] But it is perhaps Lassus who has most forcibly examined these ideas in a series of essays and in a variety of design interventions. If, as a painter, Lassus had been adept at presenting objects in a visual field that had no third dimension, as a landscape architect he was required to work with foreground, middle ground, and distance; hence his interest

10. Laurie Olin, "Fields and Poppies, Berkshire, England," drawing from Laurie Olin, *Across the Open Field: Essays Drawn from English Landscapes* (Philadelphia: University of Pennsylvania Press, 2000), p. 204. With permission of the artist.

both in distinguishing tactile and visual scales and yet in his deliberate play or game of confounding them.

One essay from 1961 was entitled "Tactile Scale—Visual Scale":[9] "The tactile scale is the one in which we move, in which it is required to acknowledge ourselves with precision: to park our car, locate the stairs, and open the door. . . . Beyond the tactile scale is the visual scale, a zone in which phenomena, even if they provide us with various sensations, are only visual."[10] Lassus realized the excitements, the conflation, or even the initial confusion, of tactile and visual while visiting Stockholm harbor in Sweden, which he recounted in another essay, "Stockholm, the Landscape" of 1969 (p. 24). The visual impression of a camouflaged warship seemed to merge with its background of the Stockholm harbor, a "landscape" that, assembling various colors and shapes, allowed the insertion of other objects without the assemblage being registered as having any foreground or distance; it was, we may say, like a cubist painting. As a result, the identification of the warship and Stockholm behind it were disguised and confused, and the photograph he took of it seemed a modern, flattened image. Except that when Lassus moved closer to the ship, he realized that what had first been simply a visual impression was now something where he could, to all intents and purposes, distinguish its various elements and even touch them.[11]

But the larger issue that this experience raised was: how do landscape architects play with the tactile and the visible, with the reachable and usable versus the seen and (in some form) the iconographical?

Other interventions by Lassus at various scales allowed him to explore that original distinction. For "The Garden Game," narrated by Stephen Bann in *The Landscape Approach* (pp. 35–39), Lassus played with new forms of tactile and visual for the somewhat derelict garden of the chateau at Barbirey-sur-Ouche. Since this early garden was not to be conserved or reconstituted, the windows overlooking it were instead engraved with images taken from earlier gardenist modes at the turn of the century in 1900. These played with the spatial and the temporal, and with the visible and the tactile event of the garden: the images on the glass were both close to the spectator and touchable (yet far from him historically), whereas what was outside the window was present and immediate but only visible.

A third example actually works with actual things, near and far: stand-

11. The belvedere in the shape of the Tour Magne, and the miniature of it, with Nîmes in the distance. Photograph by the author.

ing on a steel belvedere in the rest area of an *autoroute* in the south of France (Figure 11) we see the city of Nîmes in the distance. The near belvedere takes the shape of the famous Roman Tour Magne, though its original is some kilometers away in the city. But inside the belvedere is also a marquette of that same ancient structure. We can see the city in the far distance, even pretend to discern or imagine its most famous Roman edifice, but we can actually both touch the model itself and see the steel outline of the Tour Magne close by. We see them, certainly, but to our touch they are much more potent.

In another example, Lassus plays with the near and the far by depicting a series of abstract landscapes on the outside walls of a fairly uninteresting housing development in Uckange, France (Figure 12). What is in the foreground, the building, contains on its flat surface illusions of a countryside beyond, though now these appear on its façade. These imagined landscapes discovered among the apartment buildings have inspired its inhabitants, who had fled the uncongenial estate, to be tempted again into these blocks of flats: the painted illusion of distant landscapes brought them back, fascinated by the distant landscapes but also, in a manner of speaking, able to touch the building and even identify their apartment by the proximity of their own windows to such and such a tree or temple in the painted imagery of the façade. And in a curious way, having first despised the building, they could now touch it and, being seduced by the faraway landscape where they now return to live, they might experience the spaces in between.

LASSUS'S INNOVATIVE approach to issues of the near and the far in his designs and writings takes on larger concerns for landscape architects. Though designers may not see the theme of near and far in precisely the terms that Lassus explores, they are confronted with a series of similar topics, which can be explained as follows:

1. What the designer works on right here, in front of him, on his computer or drawing board, is also envisaged in his mind, in his own experience of places elsewhere, in books, notes, and so on, and in its significance or proposed meaning, which does not lie in the work directly in front of him. Thus the designer's work is near to him; the rest, far away: his task is to dialogue between them.

2. What is on the architect's site and what that site can intimate about it that need not be on the site—maybe its reference to locality, to what is "represented" there but is in fact to be found elsewhere—become the meaning and theme of his design.

3. Not space now, but time: the short term and the long term of thinking, walking, building. What the designer thinks as he or she works may rely upon things he or she recalls from the past, or upon how the finished work may manifest a future; equally, while the site itself is being constructed, other ideas

12. Bernard Lassus, painted façades on apartment houses in Uckange, France.

intervene to shape it. So, too, for visitors to a site once completed, there will intervene ideas that come to them while they explore it but that are not present in it.

    4. But there is also the question of what might *interrupt* our thinking and doing between the nearness and the faraway for both designers and visitors. How do we negotiate *between* something to be touched and something only visible, *between* our physical movements and our thinking? What hiatuses, what frustrations, what interruptions—good and bad—intervene?

This final item of the agenda introduces us, then, to *interventions* between the immediate (touchable) and the distant (visible): physically, that could mean elements in the landscape like hedges, walls, or ha-ha's, which interrupt our walking through and looking at landscapes; but mentally it also involves how we think about the site as we walk, or work upon its design. Gardens especially are not simply our responses to specific items—this statue, that arcade, such and such topography and the hardscape of steps or terracing— but how we think about things in between them, perhaps as we move between them, or navigate a site in the mind's eye as we strive to recollect it afterward.

If we return briefly to Lassus's examples, his own movement around Stockholm harbor allowed him to ponder what emerged as he walked, irrespective of its specific elements; the visitors to the Burgundy garden had to *connect* imaginatively what they saw and touched; at Nîmes, while touchable and visible were both at hand, the visitors had to adjudicate their relationship; and at Uckange the inhabitants needed to relate their specific building and their own apartment with a distant (and abstract) pastoral landscape. So in each case, it is what emerges as we respond to the site that shapes, even if it does not also color, the scene.

Spaces in between are not unexpected. Between figures and ground, between concentration on something nearby and our awareness of its larger context, we are all aware of these spaces. But they require, surely, a different kind of perception and reflection.[12]

IT HAS always seemed odd that we tend as landscape critics to focus upon what can be seen, touched, and talked about, drawn, or photographed in a landscape; even the distance tends to be focused upon some object, at which we might eventually arrive (see, for example, Figure 32). We can always find something to say about a statue, its subject matter and its location, and we tend to record those moments and use them in discussing gardens and landscapes. But what do we do—because we tend *not* to photograph them—with the literal "places in between" them? Take three images (Figures 13–15), all of very specific moments on three sites: Bomarzo (Italian sixteenth century), Rousham (English eighteenth century), and Little Sparta (Scottish twentieth century). In these photographs we are not invited to see some special item, no sculpture or inscription in close up, nor any distant view. These images are simply of places in between what otherwise we talk about, touch, sketch, or photograph. Two of them are images of paths, for this is easier to offer the reader here; yet any path that an individual takes in a garden, whether marked or not, would serve my argument (equally a view taken across a pond where we cannot walk).

Now what the photographs cannot show here are what even writings fail to reveal—smells, sounds, whatever surface one is walking on (gravel, paving, moss, grass), the simultaneity of sensations (the awareness of the air and breeze), the time of day and of season, and our natural ability to observe a landscape in a wide-angle gaze (we don't always look through the confined viewfinder of a camera).[13]

It is these elements that we need to involve in our discussions of gardens, however difficult it is to do this without falling into the sentimental blither and coziness of "green fingers" garden writing. As we proceed through a landscape our focus inevitably changes: suddenly or imperceptibly things become important, things to be noticed (even if they are not as palpable as a statue or inscription). Nothing in our ordinary human experience should be insignificant, but in a designed place everything *is* significant. We have only the issue of understanding what that significance could be. Our movement through a site is also a movement in our mind. Sometimes we watch carefully where to put our feet (stepping-stones in a pond), but at others our feet find their own way while our eyes and minds are elsewhere. We ignore at our peril this varied and scattered attention. It repays attention to what the Canadian literary critic Northrop Frye proposed about understanding a play: our "progress in grasping the meaning is a progress, not in seeing more *in* the play, but in seeing more *of* it" (my italics).[14]

But gardens and landscapes, even the busiest ones—like Versailles or Wang Shi Yuan (Master of the Nets) in Suzhou—always have moments

13. Bomarzo, Italy.
Photograph by Emily T. Cooperman.

when our attention is focused, not on specific items, but on others things that doubtless promote other ideas. The problem here is precisely how we record or talk about these, while not neglecting the whole. Ian Hamilton Finlay, one of whose designs is photographed here (see Figure 15), calls attention to "a lot of rhetorical space between the individual features" of gardens.[15] By this, he means the verbal and visual rhetoric, what we muse about between specific iconographic items. We need to accept all these places in between the sculptures and the temples, the interstices of the garden's mixed media, what a Japanese poet called the "many things . . . brought to my mind / As I stand in the garden / Staring at a cherry tree."[16] The difficulty, I suspect, is that we tend to generalize, think similar things in different places, whereas it is (as the poet writes) the specific cherry tree that brings to mind many things, and in other gardens there will be alternative triggers and prompts for our mind. Hegel even said that the more that thought and language enter into our representation of things, the less they retain their "naturalness, singularity, and immediacy";[17] so, too, of garden experience itself, and especially garden experience in a specific place. Yet on the other hand, we cannot rely simply, if at all, on what the eighteenth-century

14. Rousham, Oxfordshire.
Photograph by Emily T. Cooperman.

writer Joseph Addison appealed to in gardens—a "natural" aptitude "to fill the mind with Calmness and Tranquility,"[18] for that can be too anodyne and ultimately mere sentimentality. We need, in short, to attend to what happens in a specific place, with specific people, and probably at a specific moment.

THIS IS where the ways in which our explorations or promenades are structured become crucial. While we explore, we are confronted not just with paths but with walls or hedges that shape our response to sites, partly by refusing any deliberate view of other items. In 1747 when William Gilpin (later

15. Little Sparta, Scotland.
Photograph by Emily T. Cooperman.

to become famous for his picturesque descriptions) described in *A Dialogue upon the Gardens . . . at Stow in Buckinghamshire* how two friends explored those gardens, one of them was struck by what seemed an unnecessary and "impertinent" hedge. Yet his companion observes that, as with an orchestra or band, a "full pause" in the music (or the parkland) allows you the better to appreciate what surrounds it (pp. 11–12). We do not need to be "cloyed" with every item we encounter.

Similarly with these same visitors' observations of the ha-ha (p. 52) that surrounds Stowe gardens (the ha-ha, or ditch, was probably of military provenance or perhaps a means of preventing wolves from leaping into gardens, the French *saut de loup*). The ha-ha prevents visitors from moving into and touching elements in the larger landscape, while at the same time allowing them scope to explore the wider and rural landscape visually. And even before the advent of the ha-ha, visitors could still be stopped by the *claire-voie* or grills that terminated a garden path yet still allowed glimpses of the countryside outside.

HEDGES, WALLS, and ha-ha's (and there are many similar effects or impediments also in urban landscapes) are physical structures. But just as often we are stopped in our tracks by something not so palpable: for this, we could invoke a literary term, the caesura, which signifies a meaningful break within a line of verse, where we pause in reading the actual words, or when we reach the end of a line and perhaps hesitate before continuing with the next. The reader here might try speaking the famous soliloquy of Hamlet and seeing where his or her pauses occur (I have marked this for my own reading): "To be \ or not to be \\ that is the question // Whether 'tis nobler in the mind / to suffer / The slings and arrows of outrageous fortune // Or to take arms \ against a sea of troubles / And by opposing \ end them. // To die \\ to sleep No more." The caesura is, if you like, a hinge (what the French call a *charnière*) between the evidences of art, whether in verse or landscape, and our human concerns and attention.

THE MODERNIST response to what we might call the picturesque "dilemma" (how *not* to design landscapes as if they were paintings) was to turn the "painting" on its head, not just by flattening it like a cubist image, but by entering into (trespassing into) its conventional format of foreground, middle ground, and distance, and inverting it—finding the distant visible now as the nearby touchable, and as a consequence being able to focus on the spaces that come between them as we walk or meditate and where we are often confronted with disruptions in any smooth promenade.

We might conclude with two apt and related emblems. A summer cover for the *New Yorker* magazine depicted a lady on the beach. Her feet were planted on the brown sand, and behind her the blue ocean stretched to the horizon; but her hand rested on the drawn line or edge of the far horizon, as if it were a balustrade. She was both here and there, touching the sand with her feet and the far oceanic horizon with her hand. Thinking of this moment, she was "mastering" the places in between.[19]

The Japanese word "ma" has no synonym in English, but it stands for that space between gate pillars where the sun shines through (the character itself shows gateposts with the sun between them). It is not emptiness, nor what we'd conventionally call a void, but a physical space: it has been explained as the place between two or more things and events, as a "gap, opening, space between, time between, and so forth."[20] Both the Japanese character and the term help us to comprehend how a "void" is something that connects and triggers meditation on what is necessarily part of the whole. Looking at the sun between gateposts is a challenge.[21]

Chapter 3

Stourhead Revisited
and the Pursuit of Meaning in Gardens

One of the most famous English landscapes, Stourhead, provides an opportunity to examine a range of responses to it, both modern and contemporary, and then to explore how we understand what a landscape might mean, what insights it allows and encourages. The materials to be invoked here are rich, even confusing, and offer a variety of approaches to how designed landscapes communicate their meanings and how visitors choose to interpret what they discover in them.

Readers . . . who are no readers at all . . . find themselves ill at ease, unless they are let into the whole secret from first to last.
—Laurence Sterne, *Tristram Shandy,* volume I, chapter 3

The fundamental critical act . . . is the act of recognition, seeing what is there, as distinct from merely seeing a Narcissus mirror of our own experience and social and moral prejudice. Recognition includes a good many things, including commentary and interpretation.
—Northrop Frye, "On Value Judgements," *The Stubborn Structure* (1970)

THE ISSUE OF meaning in gardens and designed landscapes has preoccupied many critics over the past twenty years. Their reflections are basically of two kinds: general and conceptual reflections, on the one hand, and attempts, on the other, to explore the issue of meaning in the case of one specific site. The more general discussions of meaning may occasionally invoke actual gardens (it is, after all, rather useful to test generalizations against particular instances!), but they have been more concerned to establish principles and criteria for ascertaining what designed sites, generally considered, can mean.[1] Stourhead is, however, one particular site that has elicited a considerable and extended scrutiny which is also instructive about the more general issue of how the topic of meaning(s) in gardens might be approached.[2]

An iconic, even canonical garden of the later eighteenth century in England, a classic case of the picturesque or landscape garden, Stourhead has elicited interpretative writings by a distinguished range of scholars and garden historians. So it offers a useful means of approaching the issue of meaning(s) in garden art and landscape architecture. It cannot be said that all these endeavors—either general or specific—have produced a very satisfactory outcome, or indeed resulted in much clarity or consensus. And in March 2006 the torrent of writings on Stourhead merged with the stream of more general discussions of meaning in an article by Jane Gillette. It often seems that confusion is worse confounded when somebody attempts to straighten the record. *Caveat lector.*

Only one writer is much concerned with the physical development of the garden. James Turner saw this as having two separate stages, though both derived from an original series of ponds in the valley below the mansion. First, in the 1740s, was what James Turner, using a drawing by C. W. Bampfylde as his guide, sees as a rectangular[3] piece of water directly below the Temple of Ceres (as it then was) with a river god in a niche out of which flowed the waters of the locally named Paradise spring; there were other "formalized" bodies of water. Only from 1754 did the garden receive the shape that we now recognize (Figure 16), with its extensive and irregular lake created by a new dam to the southwest, and with other temples and insertions that included the medieval Bristol Cross, the stone bridge near the parish church, a grotto, and Alfred's Tower on the ridge to the northwest of the lake. The banker Henry Hoare (died 1725) who had built the mansion had passed the estate to his son, also Henry (but known as "the Magnificent"), who was responsible for creating the Stourhead landscape as we have it; a grandson, Colt, also took an active interest in the site.

16. The view of the lake and Pantheon at Stourhead, as first seen by modern visitors. Photograph by the author.

The outlines of Stourhead interpretation were sketched by Christopher Hussey and Edward Malins, but it was Kenneth Woodbridge who devoted himself to extensive research and publications on Stourhead and established the detailed approach that has been so influential. Like Malins (1966, p. 51), Woodbridge invoked the Claude Lorrain painting *Coast View of Delos with Aeneas* and, like Hussey (1967, p. 158), he saw the site as having a "closed circuit." But upon these foundations he proposed a rather more elaborate structure that relied upon quotations from different books of Virgil's *Aeneid* that appeared in the garden in order to propose a cluster of other Virgilian allusions and make the circuit of Stourhead a parallel to the journey of Aeneas and his founding of Rome. Thus the lake itself becomes Avernus, the River God in the grotto becomes the Father Tiber of *Aeneid* VIII, the grotto a version of Hades (based upon a calculated misreading of a private letter of Henry Hoare's, but needed to maintain the parallel with Virgil's epic), the Pantheon a symbol of ancient Rome, and the Temple of Apollo a recollection of Augustus. Ronald Paulson took this further, escalating the travels of Aeneas into "a parable of the Christian soul's journey through life" (1975, p. 30), while Max F. Schulz (1981) found Stourhead an emblem of the imagina-

34

tive redemption of the Fall of man. Meanwhile Turner had also proposed a holistic interpretation that is, however, based upon a different route around the lake, starting from the mansion (which would have been a local departure point for visitors to the house) and descending first to the grotto, and then relying almost exclusively on one inscription from the first book of the *Aeneid,* where the harbor scene described there is declared to be "topographically far closer" to that of Stourhead than any sources in Pliny or Claude that others had proposed (1979, p. 74).

In 1983 Malcolm Kelsall tried very usefully to clear up confusions from two decades of writing on the garden and its meaning, but he inadvertently managed to add some of his own and failed to acknowledge earlier suggestions upon which his own reading nevertheless drew. His main complaints, trenchantly advanced and with impressive scholarly support, were that suggestion and supposition had hardened into fact and assertion not only from one author to another but even within one piece of writing: more specifically, that the Virgilian references within the garden do not come "in the right order" to sustain the parallel with Aeneas; that the eighteenth century did not read Virgil's epic as a Christianized allegory; that Stourhead "lacks any clear reference, visual or verbal, to the founding of Rome" (1983, p. 137), and that anyway to "construct a garden to emblematize the founding of a city" is "a contradiction in terms" (p. 137). Kelsall also found the parallel with the Claude painting in no way as "exact" as previous critics had claimed (e.g., Malins 1966, p. 51), yet he nevertheless used a feature of it—a distant tower that nobody else had noticed—to sustain his own analysis. His reading puts a contemporary political construction upon Henry Hoare's garden, reminding us that Hercules was identified (but in the Renaissance) as a model of "civic virtue" (all those labors), sees a dialectical relationship between past and present and between classical and Gothic references (thus very importantly drawing into the discussion such Gothic elements as King Alfred's Tower [Figures 17a and 17b] on the hillside above the gardens, which all other critics except Turner had ignored), and introduces the themes of natural religion and Christian humanism. During the course of his reappraisal Kelsall invokes the motif of the Choice of Hercules, praising Paulson for his earlier "sensitive and perceptive" handling of the theme, as a means of explaining the rugged pathway that leaves the lake and reaches the hillside where the "Apolline temple of virtue" is (1983, p. 140). But this excursus is less convincing than his other proposals, if only because the Choice demands an actual topographical layout to correspond to the Herculean story, and this we do not have (well, we do, but its path of vice would lead to the parish church!). The same complaint, as will be seen, goes for Michael Charlesworth, both of whose articles extend the Hercules motif to rectify what he sees as earlier interpretative inadequacies. These accounts represent the core readings of the meaning of Stourhead.

Several preliminary observations will be in order here. Interpretations of Stourhead tend to be determined by the academic origins of those who offer commentaries; this is also true of the more general essays, where both designers and philosophers have featured prominently. Those who are primarily writers and literary critics (Paulson, Turner, Schulz, Kelsall, Gillette) are invariably drawn toward discursive explanations of Stourhead, seizing the verbal clues actually located in the garden itself as the authority to treat the whole: Turner explicitly states that the "textual structure" of Stourhead is "as much part of the garden as hills and temples ['its physical structure']" (1979, p. 70). Those with visual or art historical expertise or inclination (Woodbridge, Charlesworth, Ross, but also Paulson as a literary critic invading art historical territory) look to iconographical approaches,[4] which themselves usually proceed from visual clues to verbal explanations if only because their conclusions are articulated in words. What is fascinating about these interpretations of Stourhead, whether from people who have largely a visual bias or those who bring literary skills to bear, is that an "iconographical" approach seems necessary to almost all of them and yet is not an approach that any one of them feels obliged to defend. The contributions of art historians to the refashioning of garden history in the mid-twentieth century, especially when it concerned Italian Renaissance designs,[5] have doubtless made this inevitable, as have the demands of literary critics to "read" a garden.

But a garden is neither a painting nor literary text, even if some maintain that it is "almost literally a poem" (Paulson 1975, p. 30). As Charlesworth remarks in a slightly different context (2003, p. 269), when we read an inscription from Virgil on the Temple of Flora/Ceres (Figure 18) we do not necessarily, if at all, locate ourselves immediately within the context of his

17a and 17b. Stourhead, (left) King Alfred's Tower on the hillside above the garden and (right) a detail of Alfred's statue and its inscription. Photograph by the author.

poem—we are, in fact, within a garden when we read the Latin line; yet the instinct of most literary commentators is to tell us immediately the literary context of a given inscription.[6] The garden-ness of a garden is occasionally invoked,[7] especially by those who are suspicious of literary and art historical approaches; but such invocations are used mainly to ward off the possibility of meaning—a favorite move by design critics—rather than prompt explanations of meaning that might be specific to garden art. Turner betrays his refusal to think in garden terms when in the segment of the lake circuit between Ceres/Flora and the grotto he can find only "blankness," "insipidity," and indecisiveness (1979, pp. 70 and 72); but even if there is no insertion in this stretch of the lakeside circuit designed to trigger mental associations, surely the physical structure still survives and preoccupies the visitor (Laurie Olin actually sketches alongside the lake in that stretch, which suggests he was enthralled by something there).[8]

Another preliminary issue concerns the undefended assumption by both literary and art critics that Stourhead is to be grasped "as a whole," and that the "whole picture" (Charlesworth 2003, pp. 264 and 276)[9] can somehow be made apparent to us either on site or retrospectively via their commentaries. Turner observes that the "task of the garden historian is . . . [to] account for Hoare's entire creation" (1979, p. 70). The narratives that Paulson, Schulz (1981), and Turner find in the Stourhead landscape try to be resolutely coherent, "like an allegory, with a beginning, middle and end" (Paulson 1975, p. 29), even though they entail ignoring key items in the gardens—Paulson says the Gothic elements added in the 1770s are "irrelevant" (p. 29), Schulz floats happily above most actual events on the site so we do not actually know what stimuli he is including, while Turner denies significance to any inscriptions that do not pertain to the first book of the *Aeneid*, though he inclines toward reducing an emphasis on allegory (1979, p. 71, n. 16). Charlesworth, however, bases his new, holistic approach upon the (correct) recognition that Woodbridge fails to involve more than half of the lakeside journey in his explanations (2003, p. 268).

This assumption of, or search for, unity, for wholeness, in any explanation of the site's meaning, doubtless follows from these authors' training to read poems, novels, or paintings as complete and coherent works of art that add up to more than the sum of their details.[10] But it is not an assumption that works well for gardens. Gardens and landscapes are constructed over time, with

18. The Temple of Flora (previously dedicated to Ceres), Stourhead. The site of the original grotto can be glimpsed below the bank. Photograph by the author.

new insertions of both plants and buildings not necessarily observing or even having knowledge of an original sense of the whole; there is also the "insertion" into the garden of visitors in many later generations, whose responses might complicate any search for holistic readings.[11] Furthermore, there were too many items in the gardens that do not get involved in any analysis that claims completeness. While Turner is almost alone in considering the temporal development of the gardens at Stourhead, that recognition is overtaken by his determination to find a specific "textural structure" in the later physical layout. Furthermore, while we read verbal works sequentially from start to finish and, with paintings, have the whole thing in most cases before our eyes, a garden is not so available. Maybe there is only one way round this particular "closed circuit" garden, though Turner initiates the visit at a later point than do others; the lake at Stourhead certainly encourages or even imposes such an exploratory logic—except that nobody has been puzzled why all commentators assume that this circuit is to be taken in an anticlockwise (nonwestern) direction.[12] But most gardens can be explored along a variety of routes;[13] an equivalent process for novels and paintings of this varied if not random visitation might be to shuffle loose pages of a novel like cards, deal them, and then read them, or to cut up a painting (better, its reproduction!) and play with different collagist formats.[14] Yet Charlesworth claims that our arrival at the Temple of Apollo (Figure 19) provides the "climax" for Stourhead (Paulson also uses "climax" for this feature [1975, p. 29]), and that the view from there provides us with "the whole picture" (2003, p. 276). But by Charlesworth's own account that is not true—for we have not yet reached the Bristol Market Cross (which prompts him to say excellent things about industry and mercantile probity), nor can we see the grotto from Apollo's hill or read the inscription on the distant tower dedicated to King Alfred. So the "climax" looks, in artistic terms, somewhat inefficient to say the least; the only possible meaning to give that term is a topographical one—we have reached the high point, literally, of the immediate garden. However, Hoare himself implied that the larger landscape did have a climax or, as he put it, "one Scheme [that] will Crown or Top all," that is, Alfred's Tower.[15] This would indeed have been a topographical highpoint as well perhaps as an ideological climax, but it is only Kelsall who utilizes it sufficiently in an overall reading.

Another issue, as Kelsall rightly recognized (1983, p. 133), is that often interesting speculations have hardened into fact even within the space of a single article; between articles, they have often been transformed into irrefutable assertions! Slight analogies, too, have assumed the rigor of absolute explanations. What is provoking about both these reiterated ideas and Kelsall's dismissal of them is that they *do* now contribute to responsible readings of Stourhead.[16] I have argued elsewhere that around a site's "triggers and prompts" may accrete ideas, reflections and responses that sustain a series of supposed meanings, and that this record of its reception becomes difficult to separate from the site objectively or historically considered: in fact, for good reason, I

19. The Temple of Apollo, Stourhead.
Photograph by the author.

used Stourhead as my example.[17] Clearly there are objections to this perspective, not least that it gives equal weight to or even privileges almost any later response to the garden over known or plausible historical ones. But what is at stake, beyond the validity of later interpretations of a garden (as of a poem or a painting), is the process by which people come to attach meanings to, or to believe that they discover meanings in, a garden.

Perhaps the main issue to confront is what evidence to foreground in the analysis of a garden. This has proved the crucial problem with interpretations of Stourhead, where both specific paintings, which are of course not in the gardens themselves, and literary quotations, which are inscribed on buildings (but without any identification of their source), have been made the hooks upon which to hang interpretations.

For example, we know that the creator of Stourhead had a Claude painting of Aeneas in his house as well as a Nicolas Poussin painting of the Choice of Hercules.[18] These two paintings have been invoked as the key, the "open sesame," to the garden's meaning. Yet Charlesworth (2003, p. 268) is rightly skeptical as to whether anybody who had started from the mansion in the first place (not necessarily the case for every visitor, one presumes, and certainly not the modern visitor to a National Trust property)[19] would be able to recall precisely one particular painting or another once out in the grounds. Further, those—like Woodbridge and Charlesworth himself—who invoke these paintings as keys to meaning tend to jam the lock when they insert and turn them. Claude's painting is only vaguely like the actual scene the visitor sees;[20] Kelsall rightly notes that it shows, for instance, no water between the spectator and the distant temple (Pantheon), which is the case at Stourhead; the relative positions of temple and distant view are also reversed from painting to garden (1983, p. 136). It must also be said that the scale of the temples in the Claude and in the garden are totally different. Those precise objections might be laid aside, if we want to suggest only that such a painting might well be part of the mental imagery of eighteenth-century visitors and perhaps help them respond to the scene before them (more of that later). But it is a different matter to use the painting to open up a precise Virgilian reading of the garden that would necessitate recalling not only the specific picture but also its title and subject, and, further, that would require a *subsequent* encounter with two inscriptions from Virgil's *Aeneid* to implicate, if at all, the Claudean subject matter as relevant to the garden; and who knows, by the time a visitor confronts those literary insertions the painting may no longer be recalled.

Similarly, Hercules forced to choose between vice and virtue was certainly a schoolbook commonplace in the eighteenth century, but (*pace* Charlesworth 2003, p. 279) it does not translate "precisely" into the Stourhead site. Charlesworth rightly notes that our first encounter with Hercules in the garden (there was a miniature statuette in the house) is inside the Pantheon, where his statue is placed between those of Ceres and Flora.[21] But Charlesworth never uses that particular placement to show how the Herculean decision—about which ethical path the visitor should take after leaving his temple—is reenacted "precisely" at this point in the garden visit. Yet one might elaborate upon

Charlesworth's expositional logic and argue, as Paulson essentially does (1975, p. 30) and Olin veers toward (1998, p. 270), for a closer visual parallel between the Poussin painting and the temple's placement of Hercules between Ceres and Flora and for that configuration being in its turn very relevant indeed to this particular garden. For at Stourhead there is a temple dedicated to Ceres/Flora (its name was changed sometime during the 1770s,[22] which suggests some hesitation as to which woman to celebrate or follow, even though the two were conventionally paired). Flora and Ceres could readily be connected with the Herculean choice, as Charlesworth himself sees the garden offering alternative lifestyles of "industry and application to business" on the one hand and "indolence" on the other (2003, p. 278). That alternative could readily be symbolized by the industry of harvest (Ceres) and the innocent amusements of springtime (Flora). But instead of that logical and specifically local use of Hercules's choice as applied to our general impressions of the garden, Charlesworth simply leaves the Pantheon and its Hercules statue and resumes his walk around the lake to find what he then establishes as the Stourheadean Choice of Hercules: namely, a stiff climb up the hillside to Apollo versus the easy, level path to the parish church and medieval market cross (Figure 20). Yet he misses a trick in not noticing that it was the (now-lost) Hermitage which the steep path first encountered,[23] surely a suitable retreat for the seeker after virtue. On the other hand, we might worry that his topographical symbolism privileging Apollo sits uneasily with a Christian landowner and, moreover, that to follow Charlesworth's route is to neglect a forking path immediately after leaving the Pantheon and before crossing the dammed stream, for which there is no such convenient explanation.[24]

At issue here and through the Stourhead interpretations is our determination of which item in the garden will indeed to be the open sesame for the whole. Charlesworth is typical in writing of the "function [of an inscription] . . . within the garden" (2003, p. 267) and assuming that the inscription we first encounter over the entrance to the Temple of Ceres/Flora will begin to unlock the rest so that "visitors [may enjoy] a sort of optical or even conceptual possession of the garden as a whole" (p. 277). It is an assumption that derives, as already suggested, either from literary criticism, where an interpretation of the whole is deduced from the careful analysis of fragments, or from art criticism, where the iconography is similarly treated as apparent throughout all details of a painting. Turner, another literary critic, invoking a visitation of the site

20. The Bristol Cross beside the church, Stourhead.
Photograph by the author.

that begins at the house and arrives first at the grotto with its inscriptions, uses the quotation from *Aeneid* I to open up a tendentiously coherent narrative of Hoare's vision (1979, pp. 74ff.), different from any of the others who follow the modern visitor's approach past the Temple of Ceres/Flora.

To anticipate here at least one conclusion: it seems a more useful approach to agree that we cannot privilege one trigger or prompt in a garden over another, partly because the garden does not function like a novel, poem, or painting, even if we can in this particular case be sure that there is one, "authorized" route by which to experience it,[25] and partly because our attention in the spaces of a garden like Stourhead is endlessly distracted. We may perhaps retrospectively gather together some impressions and memories and work them into a whole theme or narrative, but this is not what the critics are telling us (more of that later). And often physical or topographical space is ignored or even misread, thus calling into question the very interpretations derived from it. Kelsall rightly criticized early writers on Stourhead for ignoring the Gothic elements of the garden, from which he himself elucidates a more complex message; but the classical items also get manipulated.

When Charlesworth takes us into the grotto, his analysis depends heavily upon our seeing the Sleeping Nymph first: he deals with it at once and then writes, "The visitor proceeds to another part of the grotto to discover the river god" (2003, p. 272), and from this he deduces a *sequence* of responses to mythic and real spaces. It is in fact a very interesting and convincing proposal for how we can transfer our awareness of mythic or literary allusions into the real space of a garden experience. But unfortunately his explanation of the actual event is faulty: we have, in fact, been confronted by the River God ever since we descended into the grotto, for he is placed at the far end of the grotto corridor; so we do not "proceed" from nymph to river god, since we see the god before the nymph. Small matter, perhaps; yet the sight of the River God is probably more dramatic and more central to the experience of Stourhead—he would be the very river god who initiates the headwaters of the Stour. But above all, although it is nowadays a nonverbal item, the River God once had an inscription attached to it; this Charlesworth conveniently bypasses because his analysis requires that the statue of the River God lacks a verbal prompt ("by the time we reach the river god, monitory inscriptions have fallen away" [pp. 272–73]). Accordingly, both the sequence of experience upon which Charlesworth wants to base his reading of the garden and its historical context are flawed.

Charlesworth's omission of any reference to the historical inscription below the River God raises another, key issue: namely, the role—indeed, the very status and identity—of the interpreter or visitor. Sometimes it is assumed that the proffered interpretation is one that "a late eighteenth-century tourist" would have entertained (Charlesworth 2003, p. 265); this would apparently and plausibly mean having some knowledge of the lesson of Hercules' Choice familiar from many school texts,[26] but would (strangely) not appear to involve reading the River God's inscription that was in place at that time! In fact, Charlesworth invokes a "model reader" for the lines beneath the nymph in the grotto (2003, p. 271): this can only be somebody, like him, who is acquainted with the linguistic theories of Émile Benveniste that provide him with a very compelling analysis of how we might respond to the whole garden,[27] but which provision is unhistorical.

Throughout the Stourhead literature the only visitors who are invoked to *sustain* a specific interpretation are hypothetical; Kelsall recognizes this when he argues against the resemblance of the Claude painting to the initial view of the lake and Pantheon by noting that "no visitor of the time has left upon record" any note of such a resemblance (1983, p. 137). Visitors whose comments get cited incidentally—Pococke, Walpole, Wesley, Hazlitt—are never invoked as support for any particular reading or meaning. Indeed, even Kelsall, who is the most exigent of the Stourhead critics in his determination to read the gardens in terms of eighteenth-centutry political and cultural norms, can only appeal generally to "the eighteenth-century mind" (p. 133). Otherwise he is forced to rely upon citing texts that may or may not have been in the minds of contemporary visitors, who are, from Pococke to Hazlitt, stretched over a considerable cultural timespan. The one apparent exception to this, however, is Turner, who cites more than half a dozen contemporary accounts;[28] yet none of these is crucial to his subsequent elaboration of Hoare's "values" and conceptions of Stourhead (1979, p. 77). Even here Turner can make mistakes, in assuming that the German Hirschfeld actually visited Stourhead (he didn't, so his descriptions are based at second hand upon other writings, about which we can only surmise), and in picking and choosing cavalierly among his sources—thus the Swedish artist and landscaper Piper is claimed to be right when he depicts the River God holding an oar but is criticized for inaccuracy in another drawing (cf. pp. 75 and 72, n. 29).

Further, no modern critic faces up to the awkwardly inconsequential observations that are recorded by visitors. Horace Walpole, for instance, surely a learned antiquarian mind and accomplished tourist, thought the nymph of the grotto was a "Cleopatra."[29] The anonymous poet of "Stourton Gardens" published in 1764 seems to confuse the river god with the nymph, gives no account of how he reached the grotto (central to almost all modern versions), and reads the statue of Hercules as Augustus (a shrewd insight that Kelsall could well have used). There are indeed visitors who recount visits to Stourhead (see note 28), but they are ignored or used very tendentiously to exemplify or sustain some latter-day holistic interpretation. Where we do have a sufficient collection of visitors' accounts of other garden landscapes— for Stowe, for example[30]—they often fail to fit snugly with our own modern accounts of landscape design and significance.

The absence of "relevant" contemporary responses to Stourhead (and therefore their avoidance by critics) inevitably allows free play to the scholarship and imagination of the modern commentator, whose next best move seems to be to situate and argue for meanings discerned at Stourhead within cultural contexts that can be substantially documented. Thus the bringing forward of "new evidence" (Charlesworth 2003, p. 263) is a matter of redefining the context, enlarging or altering the intellectual parameters within which the garden's meanings are to be located.[31] Turner's strategy is also to redefine the sequence of a visit to privilege one particular inscription. So all this necessarily returns us to the problem of adjudicating how these commentaries are structured and upon what clues in the site itself their interpretations are based.

Kelsall did a majestic job of demolishing some of the wilder assumptions ("manifestly absurd" [2003, p. 137]) of the different contexts which were used by Paulson, Schulz (1985), and Woodbridge (various publications), and he did so mainly by insisting upon their rhetorical manipulations of evidence and then by asking very properly how Hoare's interest in and celebration of early English culture (the medieval market cross; the monument to King Alfred [see Figures 3, 17a, and 17b]) should be involved in our understanding of the whole site. The enlargement of the discourse was admirable and did address specific resonances of the actual site. But it is somewhat disturbing that Kelsall neglects to acknowledge that Turner, whose whole essay Kelsall dismisses out of hand (2003, p. 135, n. 6), had already made the convincing points that the "Gothic and the Classical are dramatically juxtaposed" and that this "contrast was inherent in the garden from the first" (1979, p. 71). Admittedly, Turner does nothing with this observation, though he reiterates it on several occasions. Yet the deliberate mixture of classical and Gothic architecture in English landscape gardens prior to and contemporary with Stourhead—Castle Howard, Cirencester, Rousham, and Stowe are just a few—is a hugely important aspect of those landscapes to which we can assume that many contemporary visitors would be attuned without either explicitly commenting on it or needing specific prompts other than the architectural forms themselves.

But Kelsall's attempt to set matters straight did not deter others from continuing in ways that his article might have got them to review or at least to justify, most notably when invoking an ever wider and often simply conjectural[32] set of contexts in which to situate the meanings of Stourhead. Two years after Kelsall, Schulz (1985) keeps resolutely with a vaguely devotional reading of the gardens: hermits and "old-fashioned" emblems books like Francis Tolson's *Hermathenae* allow him to suggest Hoare's addiction to "pensive solitude and occasional unrestrained acts of fancy" (1985, p. 23) in "a pristine world of nature" that is linked with a eighteenth-century fascination with new world primitivism (p. 24) and essentially sustains his theme of the late eighteenth-century re-creation of "prelapsarian Edens" like Stourhead (p. 25). Colt Hoare's laying of a gravel path around the lake between 1792 and 1798, in itself an interesting physical promotion of the obligation of the circuit, is, however, used for reasons that are not clear to show the restoration by the third generation of the Hoare family of "the old unfallen perfection of a piece of Wiltshire chalk" (p. 25). The epitaph for Henry Hoare in the Stourhead parish church also gets called upon to support such a view, without registering that its crucial phrase—"this far-fam'd Demi-Paradise"—is surely an allusion to John of Gaunt's famous meditation upon England in Shakespeare's *Richard II,* which invocation would sort better with Kelsall's insistence upon the garden's appeals to early English mythology. The one convincing move by Schulz, though somewhat thrown away at the very end (p. 26), is to remind us that the original bodies of water at Stourhead were partly fed by a spring known locally as "Paradise." The conceit had been played with by the anonymous poet of 1764—"Prepare the mind for something grand and new / For Paradise soon opens to the view!" And Hussey, too, had noted how the name of the place became Stourhead to celebrate the headwaters of the river Stour partly fed by that Paradise spring (1967, p. 160). Perhaps this piece of local lore and topography, deriving from the early layout of the garden that Turner insists upon, go a long way to sustain the idea that the gardens were held to be, however whimsically or incidentally, an English version of a lost Edenic perfection created around its own Paradise spring.

Now ALL this detailed scrutiny of the achievements, stumbles, and foibles of a set of commentators would perhaps be niggardly and negative were it not for the importance of trying to understand how gardens can, if they indeed do, mean. This is a larger theme than I can address here, where I limit myself to identifying what issues are opened up by commentaries upon the one site, Stourhead, while reserving consideration of their more general aspects for another occasion.[33]

The objection that Stourhead might itself be a special case and that approaches to it are not readily usable at other sites should surely not detain us for very long. True, the commentaries that it has elicited seem to suggest that this particular landscape is composed in ways that very specifically require our attention to the prompts and triggers the site affords historically, and to suggest as well that our formulated responses to them will constitute a meaning that is more precise and more susceptible to being articulated than would be so elsewhere. On the other hand, as long as we remind ourselves that gardens emerge out of specific cultural contexts that should define or guide our inquiries, some general principles seem to emerge, and these can in their turn be briefly tested against the case of Stourhead (yet again).

The various members of the Hoare family who made Stourhead over the years left no explicit, let alone overall, interpretations of the garden. Yet critics have consistently sought to establish what their intentions might have been; Paulson (in Kelsall's words [2003, p. 134]) "felt confident enough to summarize Henry Hoare's inner thoughts" and writes that Hoare "had a particular message he wanted his garden to convey" (1975, p. 28), while Malins (1966, p. 55) can tell us what "he must have known" about finding consolation for family bereavements in delightful scenery. But even if the Hoares had left clear indications of their thinking, we may doubt whether subsequent visitors and tourists would necessarily have that knowledge and apply it to their experiences; the National Trust could perhaps provide such a reading if it existed, but even then it would be something external to the garden itself.

It is clear, however, from fragmentary early reports as well as modern responses that when a garden such as Stourhead exerts a compelling power upon its visitors, they assume that this has a source in the garden's original creation or intention.[34] Malins, pushing beyond a dependence upon Claude and Virgil, asserts that Stourhead "may be an allegory of the journey through life" (1966, p. 54). Later writers have also found "allegory" the term of choice (Woodbridge 1974), though Turner as well as Kelsall demur. Since a garden is not a poem, a novel or a picture, it cannot be "read" in ways that those art forms can be;[35] consequently, an allegorical structure, which requires authorial guidance and depends upon a consistent equation or "analogy" (Woodbridge 1974) of local items to larger ideas, is untenable. What the garden does do, however, is present visitors with a host of architectural objects, inscriptions that are quotations from Virgil (even if not attributed), Gothic structures and other inscriptions that reference Anglo-Saxon history, and many more such inventions—all set more or less harmoniously but at different times into a contrived landscape scenery. Any one, or any cluster, or all of these together can trigger visitors' imaginations, drawing upon their previous knowledge or their instinct for storytelling; but none of them can *control* what those responses would be. Paulson himself allows items to be

significant even when they do not contribute directly to his holistic interpretation—he acknowledges temples of harvest (Ceres), of fame (Pantheon),
and wisdom or the arts (Apollo).[36] Quotations, for instance, like those at the
grotto or on the Temple of Flora/Ceres, do not necessarily bring into play
their original contexts, as virtually every commentator assumes. Malins says
that "evidently Henry Hoare had the *Aeneid* in mind" (p. 51) because he
chose the inscription for the Temple of Ceres/Flora; but that does not follow
at all—he may simply have liked the words for their own sake—"Procul o,
procul este, profanes" is a resounding command ("Away, away, all ye who
are profane"). We surely all quote lines, sententious remarks or bons mots
without necessarily wanting to invoke or even thinking of the whole text
from which they come.

Kelsall quite strictly, and other critics when it suits their turn, want to
base their readings of Stourhead on what contemporaries would have known
and on how they would therefore have responded. This is admirable advice,
though there are some *caveats*. (1) If the garden continued to be developed over
many years, what "contemporary" ideas are relevant? (2) What are we to do
with several recorded remarks and responses—Wesley's attack on classical deities, for instance, or Walpole's identification of Cleopatra in the grotto—that
do not advance any modern reading and are therefore left aside but are still
part of a contemporary context? And above all (3), how do we know that any
one contemporary idea was in the mind of a Stourhead visitor and, moreover,
played a part in his or her response to the garden? In fact, we don't. Kelsall says,
for example, that it's illogical to associate a garden with the founding of a city
like Rome and that Virgil's poem was never read in the eighteenth century as a
Christian parable. His remarks may indeed be true as far as published records
and even known journals and memoranda are concerned; but unhappily the
argument does not ensure that some associations, as illogical or "absurd" as
those he rejects, would not have guided some visitor through the site. And
there are other possible allusions[37] and associations not recorded in contemporary accounts that modern commentators have still plausibly suggested might
have been in the minds of earlier visitors or even of the Hoares themselves:
Hussey (1967, p. 159), following a suggestion of Georgina Masson's, cites Pliny's
description of the sacred spring at Clitumnus as an inspiration for the whole
design, and Malins (1966, p. 50, n. 2) thinks a passage of Ovid on Pergusa in
Sicily might be a better gloss upon Hoare's overall program.

Those two very plausible suggestions open up some fundamental elements of eighteenth-century English *mentalité* every bit as resonant as Virgilian epics, Claudean landscapes, or Herculean choices and perhaps even more relevant than those topics to such a contemporary landscape as Stourhead. These are the theories and practice of associationism, on the one hand, and of *ekphrasis*, on the other (see Chapter 4). Neither has ever been discussed by commentators on Stourhead, even those who invoke the "eighteenth-century mind." Yet to think of Pliny's ekphrastic description of a sacred Roman landmark or of Ovid's equally verbalized version of an actual geographical site and to associate them with experiences at Stourhead would have been (and still probably are) commonplace habits of response. They involve two cultural practices and assumptions: the first concerns explanations of how the mind works in its response to and assimilation of sensory experience, and the second treats of how we communicate in words what we have in "the mind's eye" (our modern phrase is a useful reminder of these procedures). In terms of Stourhead and its meanings, these interlocking assumptions address the range and extent of associations provoked by the various items and the landscape in which they are discovered, and then the means by which those imaginative and mental experiences are made available, translated, and so communicated via both verbal and graphic means. This continues to be the case with all modern critics who articulate their Stourhead experiences. And the graphic articulation of experience—painting, sketching, photographing—has also always been a part of the experience of landscape; sometimes, and for some people, visualizing experience is easier than describing it in words. Yet visual renderings of Stourhead rarely seem to be invoked in discussions of its meaning; yet when they are, we engage yet again in the ekphrastic turn.

While associationist explanations may not without modification serve modern psychology, I suggest that they are still a means by which to grapple with meaning in a landscape like Stourhead. Along the route of this analysis, we have seen various items invoked as the key to unlock the garden's meaning and to "possess the garden as a whole"; but there were and are in fact many, many challenges to one's attention and many distractions, too, from any concentrated effort to grasp some unity. The visitor then and now is confronted with recollections of Claude Lorrain and Nicolas Poussin, memories of Virgil, local knowledge (of Paradise spring), reading knowledge of Latin (or maybe just the recognition of an antique tongue speaking unknown words), recognition of the *paragone*, or competition, between Gothic and classical architecture, or of the juxtaposition of parish church and neo-Roman temples, understandings of mercantile society and their now discarded medieval crosses, knowledge of classical figures like Aeneas, Hercules, Ceres, Flora, and Apollo or English heroes like King Alfred. And if those triggers and prompts were not enough, there are or were a wooden Chinese bridge that once shortened the visitor's walk around the northern end of the lake, a statue of Neptune, a Turk- ish Tent, a Hermitage with stained glass from Glastonbury, a Gothic Orangery, a Chinese Alcove, the Gothic Cottage (that survives between the grotto and the Pantheon), and a "Chinese" umbrella that was sketched by the Swedish visitor Piper. All of these at one time or another played their role in stimulat- ing a visitor's imagination as he or she walked around or as the visit was medi- tated upon subsequently; in part or in whole they constitute exactly what that "late eighteenth-century tourist," whom Charlesworth invokes (2003, p. 265), would have confronted and from which he or she would have "put together," had the visitor wished, an idea of the place.

Add to these specific prompts the very elements that enable and provide a setting for those encounters—the topographical grading of land, the floating of lakes, and above all the plantings—and the visitor is offered an extraor- dinarily rich mix to experience at one time, with distractions of one sort or another constantly occurring. Yet from this full repertoire the visitor pulls his or her special idea of the whole—it can remain in the mind or, more likely, it will issue forth in words and/or images. We see this process more clearly at Stowe: when William Gilpin published his visit to the gardens there only a few years before Stourhead was given its second remodeling, he cast it as a *Dialogue*: for the simple reason that that is how a site got "put together" by people (he gave us just two) discussing in words what each derives from their fairly divergent experience of the place. Even earlier, in 1739 Jacques Rigaud's engravings of people seem to be responding to the rich array of stimuli in Lord Cobham's gardens, which are another (visual) account of diverse reception.

But a far better literary parallel than Gilpin is Laurence Sterne's novel *Tristram Shandy*, famous above all for its conviction that a story is not "as plain and as smooth as a garden-walk."[38] If we are looking for historical ways of understanding visitors' responses to Stourhead, then this novel, written and published during the very years of the creation of that landscape, may yield most useful hints. It plays lovingly, continuously, and seriously with contemporary psychological explanations of the mind's workings, above all with "association of ideas" (I.4), and with encouraging its readers to adjudicate "the succession of our ideas" (III.18) for their aptness and usefulness. It also addresses the play between verbal and visual languages and their different abilities at translating concepts and experiences.[39]

These themes can help to elucidate the many stimuli that the Stourhead landscape provides for each visitor, who may then translate (or not, of course) those encounters into some coherent "whole." Reading the novel also enacts the simultaneity of observation and reflection that is equally necessary in the gardens, where lots of information is available without any precise directions on how to imbibe, sort, or otherwise use it. Actively encouraged by Sterne in his persona as Tristram, even as we begin reading (as in entering the garden), we start putting together some version of the whole without waiting for the false luxury of retrospection to become available. In this Sterne also plays with his role and responsibilities as an author who seeks from an accomplished and attentive reader a major role in putting together the story of Shandy's life and opinions; this reader sometimes loses his or her way but sometimes can be more accomplished even than the "author" himself: "The truest respect which you can pay to the reader's understanding, is to . . . leave him something to imagine" (II.11). That *Tristram Shandy* is "unfinished" (locally—the blank, black, or marbled pages; but also overall, petering out in volume 9) only pushes some readers, now turned literary critic, to devise explanations for the "whole." To which Stourhead provides an ironic parallel: in that its hesitations, blank spaces, and insistent prompts, its treacherously closed circuit of meaning (that actually ignores Six Wells Bottom leading to the all-important Alfred's Tower), and its possible digressions all tempt and repulse our search for meaning, both while we are visiting and even afterward in retrospection. To quote Sterne: "My work is digressive, and it is progressive too,—and at the same time" (I.22); or again, the visitor "will have views and prospects to himself perpetually soliciting his eye, which he can no more help standing still to look at than he can fly" (I.14). And this "strange combination of ideas, the sagacious Locke, who certainly understood the nature of these things better than most men, affirms to have produced more wry actions than all other sources of prejudice whatsoever" (I.4). People tend to get a handle on things—whether a novel or garden—as it "suits their passions, their ignorance or sensibility."[40] It follows perhaps that all associations, all "sudden starts, or a series of melancholy dreams and fancies" (I.2) that have visited Stourhead's visitors and critics, have some place, some validity in the garden's profuse and intricate whole: indeed, "nothing that has touched me," writes Tristram, "will be thought trifling in its nature, or tedious in its telling" (I.6).

It is clear that to introduce *Tristram Shandy* into the discussion of Stourhead's meanings is to follow other critics in invoking a fresh contextual approach as a prelude to reorienting ourselves vis-à-vis the garden's meanings. But it has the advantage of responding to both a historical condition (the much invoked eighteenth-century mind) and the actualities of the site as they were, as they changed, and as they now are. It allows for some important and obviously relevant associations—Claude, Ceres and Flora, Hercules, maybe even Aeneas—to be activated in the mind and to contribute to an experience of the garden; yet it plays down intentional or authorial explanations of the garden and instead accords some scope even to the visitor's ahistorical imagination, especially if that imagination enlarges our experience of the site. So let me conclude by returning to two, more recent accounts of Stourhead.

Stourhead appears in Jane Gillette's essay "Can Gardens Mean?" in order to sustain the argument that meaning, or what Gillette repeatedly calls "cognitive component" or "cognitive element," is wholly impossible in a "real garden."[41] In the course of her argument she adduces Olin's pages on Stourhead in his book *Across the Open Field*, which are rebuked for having ignored all the historical information and interpretation of the gardens (acquired Olin tells us in the library of the house itself [1998, p. 264]) once he sets off to describe his walk around the site: he slips, Gillette complains (2005, p. 94), "from a consideration of the landscape itself to historical information, a merging of his own knowledge of the site with information available to the eighteenth-century audience (or the first interpretive community)." She continues by saying that Olin "never actually articulates a personal reaction to the cognitive content [i.e., meaning] of Stourhead" (p. 94). This is somewhat astonishing in that she dismisses out of hand Olin's own sketches by saying that they show he "reacted to Stourhead considered apart from information about Stourhead," and that "we find nothing [in the drawings] that really suggests how Olin responded to the cognitive content of Stourhead—except to note that he does not address it" (p. 94).[42]

This is to confuse how transcriptions (ekphraseis) are handled differently by verbal and visual artists. Visual artists long before Olin—some of whom

21. Six Wells Bottom, featuring another medieval monument from Bristol, St. Peter's Pump, placed by Hoare in the valley leading up to King Alfred's Tower. Photograph by the author.

were illustrated by Woodbridge (1970a)—captured their impressions of specific Stourhead scenes, but modern commentators never assume that they can contribute to any meanings discerned there.[43] Artists may not necessarily be concerned with tracing a narrative or making visible some overall iconographical program at Stourhead, but from Piper to Olin they have been attracted by specific visual moments and accordingly focused upon one particular view in their graphic records. During the 1810s Francis Nicholson, for instance, chose a location in Six Wells Bottom (Figure 21) featuring another medieval monument from Bristol, St. Peter's Pump, placed by Hoare in the valley leading up to the ridge to Alfred's Tower. No commentator ever uses this image, yet the fact that it attracted Nicholson suggests that for him or others it invoked, as indeed it still does, a crucial piece of the Gothic/classical cultural debate here. Even perhaps the Turkish and Chinese items might just have had a role to play (with apologies to Kelsall for extending his perspective) in Stourhead's declaration of different cultural allegiances that Wiltshire landowners might have entertained during the long eighteenth century. Both "natural" settings and incidental artifacts, whether instantly meaningful or not, can provoke the minds and imaginations of visitors, and it is precisely the rich variety of these stimuli that we need to celebrate. Schulz begins his 1985 essay by noting that the eighteenth-century *furor hortensis* "drew its inspiration from many fonts"; this is undoubtedly true, and therefore does not encourage the isolation of any one source of inspiration for Stourhead.

So Olin, uniquely among Stourhead's commentators in using his own images alongside a discursive text, might be said to provide two different perspectives. When Gillette accuses him of slipping from his experience of the place to "historical information" (she also says he "merges" them) as he sets off around the lake, we might equally see that his visual record, in its own graphic mode, is attuned to the slippery coincidence of fact and experience in a way that recalls Sterne's explorations of the different virtues of the verbal and the visual. Olin's map of the site (Figure 22), for instance, with its waters marked in black, its wooded slopes differentiated from fields, but otherwise left eloquently without annotations, is so different from anyone else's that it returns one emphatically to the physicality of the site as well as reinforces his text's immediate recognition of "property—houses, mills, rivers, pastures, as well as traditional rights and obligations" (1998, p. 257). The textual discussion of cultural resources is aptly hinted at in other drawings, too: his view of the house front, with both an aged oak and recent planting; his view across the ha-ha to the obelisk (only Turner attends to that feature); and his very unexpected Pantheon almost lost in the deeply enfolding woods and seen across the lake past an obtrusive island from exactly the point on the lake circuit where others have found a dearth of incidents between the Temple of Flora and the grotto—all these images "speak" of a strong response to the significance of the site as a repository of various notions of Englishness (Olin's book, after all, is subtitled *Essays Drawn from English Landscapes*). His text is attentive, too, by its tone and personal inflections, to the architectural accretions to the house and other elements added to the pleasure grounds (1998, pp. 260, caption, and 275–76), and therefore to the continuities and disruptions of the historical process. These may not be pulling the "right" meaning or "cognitive" significance from Stourhead, but the experience of being there and of having immersed himself in the cultural history of the place is emphatically drawn and the two connected.

The "slippage," then, between kinds of knowledge and experience during garden visits and in garden criticism is at once unconscious and practiced,

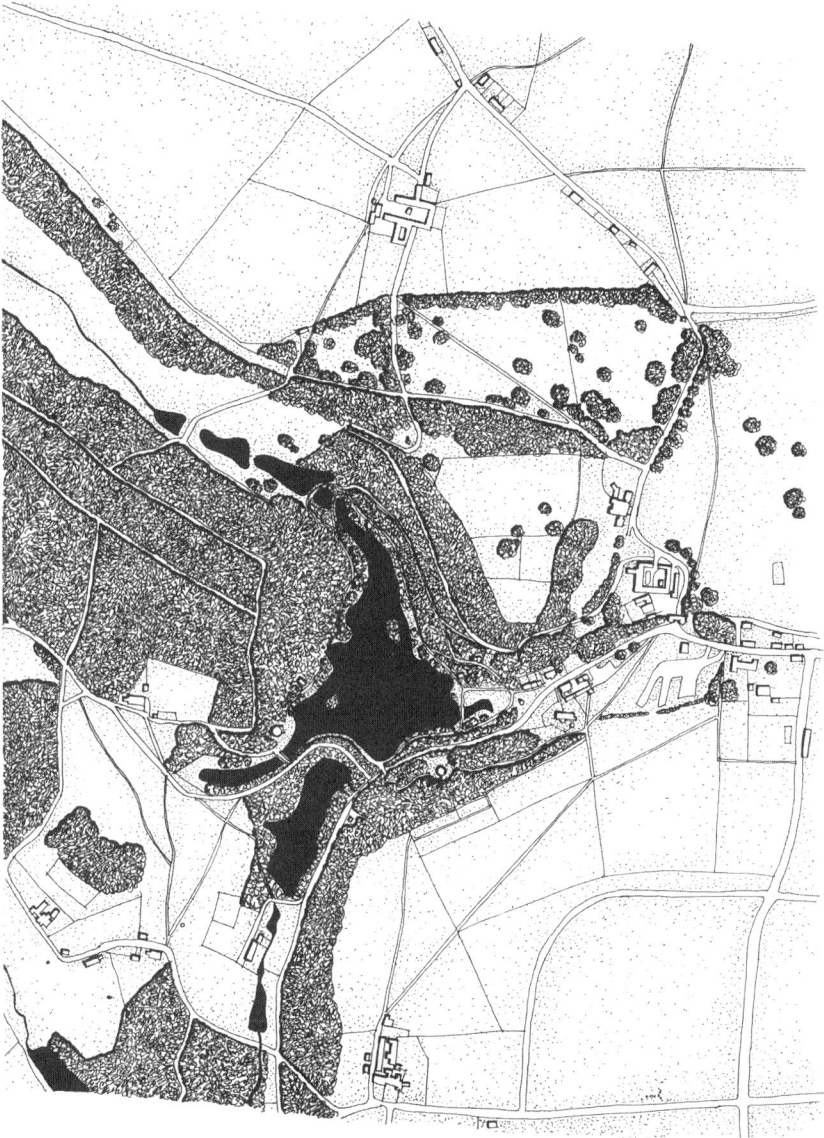

↑
N

22. Laurie Olin's plan of the site of Stourhead: the rectangular outline of the house is on the right, and the valley leading up to Alfred's Tower toward the top left. From Laurie Olin, *Across the Open Field: Essays Drawn from English Landscapes* (Philadelphia: University of Pennsylvania Press, 2000), p. 273. With permission of the artist.

fruitful and problematic. It is part of the challenge in reading gardens; working out how best to get the balance right between what we can know historically and what we feel phenomenologically. To make that double contribution integral to a consideration of gardens is the ultimate ambition of the garden critic.

So where does this leave "meaning"—in Stourhead, or indeed in other gardens? I believe that in many cases the word would be best abandoned altogether (being too contaminated by misuse), or at least refined by the occasional substitution of such terms as "significance" or "experience" for encounters that seem low in "cognitive content" but otherwise seem important. But that is another story. On this side of large and general reactions to the modern anxiety over meaning in designed landscapes, the specific case of Stourhead offers two, more limited conclusions.

The first is that that we might profit by thinking of Stourhead's structure within the context of eighteenth-century associationism (historically apt as that philosophy is), by which a sophisticated range of ideas can be linked to specific and physical encounters. How we then evaluate the associative moves that various visitors and critics make in different parts of the garden will depend in large part upon the mental and imaginative logic and agility of the mental associations themselves, upon how one association is linked to others, and above all how they are expressed verbally and visually. Of all commentators discussed here, Christopher Hussey in his pages on Stourhead seems the most attuned to (without specifically invoking) associationism: he is clearly enthralled by the place; he acknowledges allusions and historical points of reference (the lives and contacts of the Hoares, for example); he writes of specific prompts without according any of them a privileged role in his commentary; and he stops short of advancing any holistic interpretation other than his insistence on the garden's "closed circuit" (which may anyway imply just a pedestrian topography).

The second conclusion to be drawn from this consideration of meaning at Stourhead would be to take advantage of the insights afforded by the historical activity of associationism for studying later gardens or the later reception of older ones. Associationism, in short, continues to yield a useful tool for exploring garden reception. After all, a quantum shift in thinking about the human mind and imagination was engineered by British empirical philosophers following Locke's initiative, and this importantly involves associationism as a crucial part of a modernism whose watershed has been (rightly, I believe) located around 1800.[44] Garden experience is still deeply indebted to those habits of mind which once were practiced equally along the banks of the lake at Stourhead, or through the pages of *Tristram Shandy*, and which could now be transferred (one imagines) to the bright red *fabriques* of Parc de La Villette as much as to *Finnegans Wake*.

Appendix 1. Bibliography of Major Items on Stourhead

1764 A poem "Stourton Gardens," written in June 1749 and published in the *Royal Magazine* for February 1764, pp. 102–3.

1779 Anonymous, *A Ride and a Walk Through Stourhead* (London).

1965 Kenneth Woodbridge, "Henry Hoare's Paradise," *Art Bulletin* 47, no. 1, 83–116.

1966 Edward Malins, *English Landscape and Literature 1660–1840* (London), pp. 49–56.

1967 Christopher Hussey, *English Gardens and Landscapes 1700–1750* (London: Country Life), pp. 158–64.

1968 Kenneth Woodbridge, "The Sacred Landscape," *Apollo* 88, 210–14.

1970a Kenneth Woodbridge, *Landscape and Antiquity: Aspects of English Culture at Stourhead 1718 to 1838* (Oxford: Oxford University Press).

1970b Kenneth Woodbridge, *The Stourhead Landscape* (London: National Trust); revised edition published in 1982.

1974 Kenneth Woodbridge, "The Dream of Aeneas: A Rosa Source for Cheere's River God at Stourhead," *Burlington Magazine* 116, p. 756.

1975 Ronald Paulson, *Emblem and Expression: Meaning in English Art of the Eighteenth Century* (Thames & Hudson), pp. 28–31.

1979 James Turner, "The Structure of Henry Hoare's Stourhead," *Art Bulletin* 61, no. 1, 68–77.

1981 Max F. Schulz, "The Circuit Walk of the 18th-Century Landscape Garden and the Pilgrim's Circuitous Progress," *Eighteenth-Century Studies* 15, 1–25.

1983 Malcolm Kelsall, "The Iconography of Stourhead." *Journal of the Warburg and Courtauld Institutes* 46, 133–43.

1985   Max F. Schulz, "Hoare's Stourhead: An Elysium at Mid-century," in *Paradise Preserved: Recreations of Eden in 18th and 19th-Century England* (Cambridge: Cambridge University Press), pp. 22–26.

1989   Michael Charlesworth, "On Meeting Hercules in Stourhead Garden," *Journal of Garden History* 9, no. 2, 71–75.

1998   Stephanie Ross, *What Gardens Mean* (Chicago: University of Chicago Press), pp. 63, 73–76, 77–79, 178.

1998   Laurie Olin, *Across the Open Field: Essays Drawn from English Landscapes* (Philadelphia: University of Pennsylvania Press), pp. 257–76.

2003   Michael Charlesworth, "Movement, Intersubjectivity, and Mercantile Morality at Stourhead," in *Landscape Design and the Experience of Motion,* ed. Michel Conan (Washington, D.C. Dumbarton Oaks), pp. 263–85.

2003   John Dixon Hunt, *The Afterlife of Gardens* (Philadelphia: University of Pennsylvania Press), pp. 200–205.

2005   Jane Gillette, "Can Gardens Mean?" *Landscape Journal* 24, no. 1, 85–97 (specifically pp. 93–95).

2012   Oliver Cox, "A Mistaken Iconography? Eighteenth-Century Visitor Accounts of Stourhead." *Garden History* 40, no. 1, pp. 98–116.

2015   John E. Harrison, "The Development and Content of Stourhead Gardens: Recent Findings, Insights from An Eighteenth-Century Poem and the Visit of Carlo Gastone della Torre di Rezzonico." *Garden History* 43, no. 1, pp 126–43.

Appendix 2. Select Bibliography of Writings on the Meaning of Gardens

David E. Cooper, *A Philosophy of Gardens* (Oxford, 2006), specifically chapter 6.

Jane Gillette, "Can Gardens Mean?" *Landscape Journal* 24, no. 1 (2006), pp. 85–97.

John Dixon Hunt, *Greater Perfections: The Practice of Garden Theory* (Philadelphia: University of Pennsylvania Press, 2000).

Mara Miller, *The Garden as an Art* (Albany: State University of New York Press, 1993)

Laurie Olin, "Form, Meaning, and Expression in Landscape Architecture," *Landscape Architecture* 7 (1988), 149–68.

Robert B. Riley, "From Sacred Grove to Disney World: The Search for Garden Meaning," *Landscape Journal* 7 (1983), 235–46.

Stephanie Ross, *What Gardens Mean* (Chicago: University of Chicago Press, 1998).

Marc Treib, "Must Landscapes Mean? Approaches to Significance in Recent Landscape Architecture," *Landscape Journal* 14 (1995), 47–62.

Chapter 4

Thomas Whately's *Observations on Modern Gardening*

Whately's assessment of landscape reception privileges words rather than images, and suggests that our viewing of sites is a way of ensuring that our responses, our insights, allow some, but not unlimited, flexibility of interpretation; an emphasis that is echoed by his contemporary French theorist Jean-Marie Morel.

THOMAS WHATELY PUBLISHED his *Observations on Modern Gardening* in 1770 (it was published first in Dublin the same year, which makes the London edition the second). The following year a French translation of that work by François de Paule de Latapie was published in Paris with the title *L'art de former les jardins modernes ou l'art des jardins anglais*. The volume was, and still is, justly famous as a major text that explained and championed the so-called English garden style, and with versions in both French and English it enjoyed a wide readership throughout Europe, Russia, and Scandinavia.

If we consult the title page, we are struck (more so in these days of hugely illustrated books on gardens) by the phrase in the subtitle: "Illustrated by Descriptions." Indeed, the French translator wanted to use engravings for his text, but Whately (in a letter published in Latapie's introductory "Discours" in the French translation) argued that "mediocre engravings" would be far worse than "the most beautiful perspectives in nature" and therefore were to be avoided. Latapie did, in fact, himself add a map of the gardens at Stowe in his French edition.

We do not know *why* Whately did not want illustrations in his text, because it was not that there were none available in 1770 to support his work. We might assume it was a question of expense, but that seems implausible for two reasons: Whately was himself well enough connected and, as political manager or agent for George Grenville and then undersecretary of state for Lord North, surely could have found the funds. Many other texts at that time, to which I will return, utilized good engravings, yet many others where we might expect illustrations had none, so it appears hard to tell why in any one case. Whately himself died in 1772, two years after the publication of his book, and no further editions were illustrated until the sixth of 1801; so it was nearly thirty years before half a dozen engraved views were added, one of them as a frontispiece, that illustrated six canonical sites in England. Yet it must be said that these were, even as late as 1801, very indifferent images—what Whately himself to the French translator had termed "mediocre" (Figure 23). One can understand why, looking at these, Whately might well have said he would much prefer "beautiful perspectives in nature" (Latapie's "Discours," p. liii).

But that phrase is itself curious: the term "perspectives" at that date would have meant (more or less what we think of today)—the sight of, or an optical depiction of, some solid object, a visible scene, a view or a prospect: thus the garden maker John Evelyn in 1660 said that a painted view or "perspective" at the end of a garden would give the illusion that its narrow and small site was more spacious. Thus a *perspective* is about *representations* of landscape that suggest depth and the texture of natural or designed scenery, and these would mean *visual* views, as shown in the 1801 images, however mediocre, that were added to Whately's sixth edition. But we can represent things in ways other than with visual images.

For Whately's title page spoke of his text being "illustrated by descriptions." Now the word "descriptions" could only in this context mean *verbal* accounts of sites, in other words what we call "ekphrasis," from the Greek that means writing about seen things, pictures certainly, but also anything out there that we *see*: namely, verbal descriptions of any visual items (they could be paintings or sculpture, but by the later eighteenth century would also refer to scenery, both natural and designed).[1]

In fact, Whately's text of 257 pages contains fourteen ekphrastic descriptions of sites, from one page (for such sites as Esher, or Ilam, in Derbyshire)

23. Esher Place, an engraved image from Whately's 1801 edition.

to eight or nine pages on Painshill and the Leasowes; by 1770 all these were well-known landscaped sites. They amount to seventy-four pages of description. Moreover, five picturesque sites are added, like the Wye Valley and the Derbyshire Dales, equally beginning to be admired by traveling Englishmen forced to forgo their Grand Tours and explore their own countryside because of wars on the European continent. These occupy a further fifteen pages. It is a rough calculation, but a third of Whately's book is thus "illustrated by descriptions." Yet virtually all of the sites so verbally described had been the subject of engravings or even paintings (which therefore could be engraved); these include Blenheim, Claremont, Esher, Hagley, Persefield, Stowe, Woburn. So it seems clear that Whately deliberately choose to "describe" each of these sites rather than show them in engraved images. But why?

The date of Whately's volume, 1770, came at a time of considerable production of books on the English garden; some were illustrated, others not. Robert Morris's *Essay upon Harmony as it relates chiefly to situation and building* from 1739 had no illustrations; nor did George Mason's *Essay on Design* of 1768. Though the French book on the Marquis de Girardin's Ermenonville was well enough documented and was illustrated with, as its title page documents, twenty-five views, the English translation of Girardin's book as *An Essay on Landscape Architecture* in 1783 contained just one frontispiece. Other important books also eschewed imagery: including William Mason's famous and much read poem "The English Garden" of 1783 and Horace Walpole's essay on modern gardening. Walpole's very influential and wildly patriotic effusion was written sometime in the late 1750s and 1760s, but then was clearly revised by Walpole after 1770 in the light of Whately's book. It was first included in volume 4 of his four-volume survey of painting, *Anecdotes of Painting in England*; the book was printed privately in 1771 but not released until 1780, and once again in 1782. Then the essay, *The History of the Modern Taste in Gardening*, was issued separately only in 1785 and subsequently also translated into French.[2] The essay itself contained no illustrations, despite the fact that it originated in a study of English *painting;* but then verbal descriptions or ekphraseis of paintings were conventional and routine in such commentary.

In short, *either* there was for Whately a chronic shortage of cash for publications—an austerity that we are all familiar with in today's publishing world—*or* something else was at stake. And—though I cannot spend time on this—there was no shortage of garden publications between, say, 1718 and 1793 that lacked engraved imagery. So clearly something else is relevant here.

I suggest two reasons. First, there is the essential difference between words and images, of which the eighteenth century was fully aware, not least because of Gotthold Ephraim Lessing's *Laocoön* from 1766, which explored the limits of painting and poetry, or Joseph Spence's *Polymetis* of 1747 (with two more editions from 1755 and 1774), where Spence sought to teach his fellow Englishmen about Roman mythology by using both images and words. Second, this difference between the verbal and visual was expressed often as a *rivalry* between what can be said or written and what needs to be drawn or painted and therefore seen. This rivalry was regularly often announced as a *paragone*, a competition between, say, music and painting, or painting and sculpture, but the paragone also extended to the rivalry between words and images. We know this, even if we forget those differences: any landscape architect today knows to provide plans, sections, or perspectives with suitable annotations, and these had been available very early, also frequently annotated with words. And this is equally familiar in so many Chinese drawings of landscape where the image and its adjacent text work collaboratively but also in their own different ways.

So what was *different* in the way of Whately's assumption that his "descriptions" nevertheless were used to "illustrate" his account of modern "English" gardens? I think the answer lies clearly at one point in the text where he distinguished between two kinds of landscape in what he termed "character." This is a distinction I pursued many years ago in a 1971 article in the American journal *Eighteenth-Century Studies*, and it was republished in French in the publication *URBI*; I have sometimes been taken to task for exaggerating this distinction between what Whately called "emblematic" and "expressive" characters. I should say now that I never assumed that they were mutually exclusive. The issue for me was that, depending on the person observing landscape, and the landscape itself, this distinction between different characters was plausible and palpable. Indeed, Whately himself is perfectly clear that such a distinction is apparent in how one perceives landscape. What I didn't entirely realize forty-five years ago was that this was all about how the viewer, not the designer, responded to landscape; it was about the audience of sites, not about the designer's intensions for them, about what (much more recently) I have called the afterlife of gardens.

In a passage on page 151, Whately protests about what would we would call iconographical items—historical and mythological sculptures like river gods, "heathen deities," columns "erected only to receive quotations," and other "puerilities" (all his terms). He chose to term all of these "emblematical," and he found them simply "ingenious," useful and able to "recall absent ideas," but he said that—and this is the crucial point—they made "no immediate impression" on garden visitors; they were not, he said, "expressive." The emblematical stuff, he explained, needed to be "examined, compared, perhaps explained, before the whole design of them is well understood." He preferred these items to be "suggested by the scene," and he opposed that skill of suggestion to a cumbersome "allegory" that he thought was "sought for . . . [or] labored." Now much more recently Jane Gillette, writing about how we respond to gardens, thought that "allegory" was "restful," as she termed it.[3] I suspect that she means that gardens make no demands upon one, that we see the allegory and relax without worrying about what it means, succumbing to the usual and platitudinous sense that all gardens are restful, what Ian Hamilton Finlay called "retreats," not "attacks." Gillette and Whately seem to be on the same page, despite their different views of what allegory means: both are concerned with *how* we respond to gardens—Whately didn't want labored and extensive examination of gardens, and Gilette is concerned that we don't *over*-respond to gardens and rather adopt a "restful" attitude!

It is clear that Whately is referring as much to how visitors responded to gardens as to the designer's intentions in making them, and in this respect he was largely following the work of Capability Brown and before him, so he must have thought, William Kent. Certainly it was both of those designers whom Horace Walpole, writing in the 1760s but not yet publishing his essay, praised as significant modern and English designers. And Walpole, perhaps having read his Whately before publication, also protested that earlier designers (in particular George London and Henry Wise) had "stocked our gardens with giants, animals, monsters, coats of arms and mottoes" (p. 41). Yet Walpole does seem to have got ahead of himself when he bade "adieu to canals, circular basins, and cascades tumbling down marble steps" and in particular applauded "that forced elevation of cataracts was no more" (p. 45), for the Kent garden he most prized was Rousham in Oxfordshire, where Kent's own sketch shows cataracts forced into the air[4] (and if the hydrological system was still intact at Rousham, we'd see it still and be able to challenge Walpole).

It is important to note that Whately's discussion of "character" was perfectly typical, and not itself a radical theoretical advance for modern gardening. Before Whately focused on specific concepts or theories of character, his previous 150 pages had constantly invoked the idea of character in ground, wood, water, rocks, and buildings (the five key elements of landscape design); it is clear that the character of any of these inculcates an idea, gives (as he says) "scope to the imagination" (p. 72). He took up the well-rehearsed notion of character from the third Earl of Shaftesbury's *Characteristics of Men, Morals, Opinions and Times*, published during the 1710s, and that attention to character was reprised more fully in Robert Morris's *Essay in Defense of Ancient Architecture* of 1728 and *Lectures on Architecture* of 1734. I do not propose to take these matters up (they are well aired and reviewed by David Leatherbarrow in his collection of essays *Topographical Stories*). I gesture to them to show that for Whately to return to this topic in 1770 was nothing new; his concern was to address character in landscape, and its impact, its effect, and its affect on garden visitors. No wonder his book was used by many garden tourists, including Thomas Jefferson in 1776, who found that its hints on how to respond to landscapes were more important than what Whately himself derided as "botanical distinctions."

And to focus on this—what Whately called the expressive character of garden design—meant that it had to be described in words. This is precisely what he did in a sustained passage of his book, when he discussed Capability Brown's work at Stowe in the Grecian Valley (Figure 24). The Temple of Concord and Victory has been variously ascribed to other architects, including Kent and James Gibbs, as well as to Brown (for we must remember that he was also and often an architect);[5] as Brown was working on the landscaping, it is plausible that he was somehow responsible for the whole valley design. (This specific question is immaterial as regards what Whately writes, but it is

24. Stowe, the Grecian Valley with the Temple of Concord and Victory. Photograph by the author.

important to see how he describes the topographical situation and the design of the valley itself).

The Grecian Valley was a new departure for the landscaping of Cobham's estate at Stowe, where a building deliberately designed to imitate Greek architecture[6] faces a landscape largely devoid of imagery; this was an early gesture by Brown to present a molded and graded terrain for its own sake, an ideal "natural" and neoclassical beauty. There were, certainly, statues scattered on the fringes of the Grecian Valley, and—rather aptly—a temple from elsewhere in the grounds, called the Gibbs Building (after the architect), was removed and *hidden* in a glade at the top of the Grecian Valley in 1764. In relocating it, it was renamed as a "Fane of Pastoral Poetry," a term that surely denotes, instead of "temple," its outmoded notion.

Whately in 1770 responded precisely to this overall Brownian effect of temple and natural valley when, in a whole section on the Grecian Valley in *Observations on Modern Gardening,* he enthused on the situation of the site "in itself" without recourse to anything other than the play of light and shadows upon it during the day.[7] The passage is too long to quote in full, but I need to suggest that it is wholly consonant with Whately's observations on modern gardening. His passage (pp. 243ff.) dwells on the beauty of the site, on the different shapes of ground and treescape, its different lights (now dark, now obscure, now shadowed) and the tints of the foliage, on the times of day, but it says nothing about any emblematical devices therein. As Whately writes, "Some species and situations of objects are in themselves adapted to receive and to make impressions which characterize the principal parts of the day . . . [communicating] the spirit of the morning, the excess of noon, or the temperance of evening." And indeed, a year before Whately's sixth, illustrated edition was published, an image of the Grecian Valley was drawn by John Claude Nattes, which attempts to register what Whately tried to describe in words (Figure 25).

This emphasis by Whately on the effect of designs upon users, upon visitors, or upon what one is tempted to call audience, seems to be at the heart of *Observations.* He does not want to illustrate visually how a designer might work—he does not use, for example, any diagrams of how his various materials might be designed or formulated—no images of topography of ground, woodland, waters, or rocks that one might get today's landscape architeture students to draw on the basis of his descriptions. Everything he discusses points not simply to how designers would work to contrive their landscapes

25. John Claude Nattes, "The Grecian Valley," 1805, pencil and wash. Buckingham County Museum, Aylesbury. Used with permission.

(though he is categorical in his diagnosis of *how* they should work); the purpose of a designer's work is to promote what he calls "scope to the imagination" (p. 72) for those who use or respond to it. His prose therefore endlessly implies how we might react, how a design might promote a "train of thought" (p. 152). In this insistence on the train of thought or "association" he is wholly in line with the British empirical philosophy that values how minds respond to the world outside them. Thus, as so many books between 1770 and 1810 make clear, it is words that have to do that job, which illustrations cannot match, especially as they are only "representations" of the world outside the mind and in no way comparable to the reality thus imaged (he makes this point on the very first page of his book).

There is a down side to all this, of course. It privileges or promotes the idea that anyone, just anyone, can find some expression of what he or she sees: *quot homines, tot sententiae*, or as many notions as there are people. This is solipsist silliness. A modern critic, Robert Irwin, has argued that "expression" is simply meaningless, "simply the lowest commentator arising from modern art's placing the individual at the crux of the decision-making process."[8] If "expression" is, then, the basic response of anyone to a scenery, and depends not on a shared knowledge of emblematical items but on what any person chooses to find there, it leaves garden commentary in the hands of those who are able to argue most convincingly for some interpretation: we presumably all know of garden commentary that seems just dead wrong. That in turn leaves assessment to be judged on a case-by-case basis.

Now Whately acknowledged in a letter to his French translator, Latapie, that he could contemplate regularity where it was "useful"; he wrote that a regular layout to be bearable must be absolutely "necessary . . . if it is to be substituted for the freedom and variety of nature. I admit regularity in certain circumstances, to which we may add the case of a *public garden*, although it is not mentioned in the book, because it doesn't enter into my subject. Gardens of this kind form a class apart, and must be composed differently than private gardens. One would miss the point, if one did not install very large allées in straight lines." His remarks were reprinted in Latapie's introduction (p. liv), and although Whately did not specifically address the issue of character and emblematic characters there, or the use of such items as "heathen deities," inscriptions on columns and suchlike would continue to be used throughout public parks and gardens.

Now it is also useful, indeed important, to situate Whately's book, finally, within the larger European writing or theorizing on garden making. The book was published in French in 1771. Five years later, namely in 1776, the first edition of Jean-Marie Morel's *Théorie des jardins* was published. The frontispiece of Morel's second edition of 1802 (Figure 26) suggests an emphasis similar to Whately's, with its engraving of a natural landscape and cascade. Morel offers what is probably the most careful and nuanced discussion of landscape or place-making of any in late eighteenth-century Europe. It is obvious to me (though I cannot find a way to prove it definitely) that Morel must have read Whately in the French edition; it is strongly suggested if Whately's discussion of the "characters" of water is compared with the same passage in Morel.

THÉORIE DES JARDINS,

O U

L'ART DES JARDINS

DE LA NATURE.

SECONDE ÉDITION, revue par l'Auteur, enrichie
de Notes, et suivie d'un Tableau Dendrologique,
contenant la Liste des Plantes ligneuses indigènes
et exotiques acclimatées, etc. etc.

PAR J.-M. MOREL,

Ancien Architecte, Membre ordinaire de la Société
d'Agriculture, de Botanique et des Arts utiles du
département du Rhône, et de l'Athénée de Lyon.

Il entretint les Dieux, non point sur la fortune,
Sur ses jeux, sur la pompe et la grandeur des Rois;
Mais sur ce que les champs, les vergers et les bois
Ont de plus innocent, de plus doux, de plus rare.
LA FONTAINE. Fable de Philémon et Baucis.

TOME PREMIER.

A PARIS,

CHEZ LA Vᵉ PANCKOUCKE, Imprimeur-
Libraire, rue de Grenelle, Nº 321, faubourg Saint-
Germain, en face de la rue des Sts.-Pères.

AN XI. — 1802.

C'est l'art de la Nature.

26. Jean-Marie Morel, frontispiece and facing engraving
from the second edition of *Théorie des jardins*, 1802.
Author's collection.

Morel writes: "Waters in landscapes are the body's soul; they animate a scene
. . . if the waters are stagnant, if they flow slowly or advance rapidly, if they
escape energetically or tumble noisily their impressions are neither equivocal
nor uncertain. . . . The mirror of tranquil water reflects pictures that a spectator may vary at his pleasure. All these nuances, modifying their effects in a
thousand forms, furnish an infinity of resources to enriching the pictures of
Nature and vary her expression" (my translation).[9] Morel extends Whately's
thinking. As an engineer, trained at the School of Ponts et Chaussées in Paris,
he is an expert in natural landforms, surface and subsurface geology, typological formations and outcroppings, flood plains, slopes, surfaces, plant species,

and vegetation; so he offers exactly what a modern curriculum would provide for landscape students. In short, he writes in the same spirit as Whately, by insisting on exactly how we visit and understand landscapes, but also on how a landscape architect must be trained, implying how his or her education or *formation* should be directed. No wonder he urged architects to stop designing landscapes and allow landscapists do their work.

Chapter 5

John Ruskin, Claude Lorrain, Robert Smithson, Christopher Tunnard, Nikolaus Pevsner, and Yve-Alain Bois Walked into a Bar . . .

> *. . . for a* conversazione *on the* modernity of the picturesque.
> *Everybody knows Ruskin, though few read him; Lorrain was*
> *a famous painter and was responsible (though it was not his*
> *fault) for being imitated by painters and gardeners throughout*
> *the eighteenth century; Smithson, who died in 1973, was a*
> *famous land artist and writer; Tunnard, who wrote on modern*
> *gardening and tried to tie it to its previous history, taught at*
> *Harvard and Yale; Pevsner was a modernist architectural critic*
> *who was nevertheless fascinated by the picturesque; Bois is a*
> *distinguished art historian at the Institute for Advanced Study,*
> *Princeton.*

RUSKIN BEGAN BY observing, rightly, that "probably no word in the language (exclusive of theological expressions) has been the subject of so frequent or so prolonged dispute; yet none remain more vague in their acceptance." It was, essentially, a question of how the term, the word "picturesque," could or should be invoked, given its utter uselessness in the hands of journalism, a bland and empty gesture toward something undefined. So it was a debate about the word. Robert Smithson said that it had been "struck by lightning over the centuries," but that the topic had been dismissed by "timid academics"; Yve-Alain Bois concurred. Somebody mentioned Salvator Rosa, who was particularly fond of depicting tree trunks split by thunderbolts. Others in the crowd, mainly landscape architects, muttered that such aged and rotten trunks should be felled, pulped, and used for fertilizers. But the vagueness—not to say the hostility—was countered by citing certain issues from the very beginning of the picturesque in the later seventeenth century, which the present-day world had neglected.

Two related themes were raised, one etymological, the other related to the subject matter of the picturesque. Etymologically, the word had appeared first in northern Italy, and this usage was taken into English by William Aglionby's *Painting Illustrated* of 1685, where Aglionby writes that some Italian painters were "working A la pittoresk, that is boldly." This was therefore about how the artist worked—choosing relevant natural materials (scenery and even human physiognomy)—which could be represented with virile brushwork on the canvas or by the burin's excavation of and printing from the engraved plate. The imagery therefore insisted on its own artifice, on the deliberate refusal of seeing the painting as a "natural" view through a window. A similar attitude was probably in the mind of A. J. Downing in mid-nineteenth-century America, when he spoke of the picturesque as "an idea of beauty strongly and irregularly expressed." Even Ruskin, who was not fond of Thomas Gainsborough, said that Gainsborough was said to have introduced "business for the eye" into his paintings (that is, busyness, what the enthralled eye would relish in the forms of the paint and brushwork). There was general assent that the picturesque was inclined to relish the rough and unfinished in both subjects and their media; fragments were seized as part of the picturesque effect, since they reflected the effects of time, the time of both the artist's activity and the evidence of temporal disruption and decay. Fragments found in natural terrain were especially admired: Smithson said it was exactly this notion in Uvedale Price's verbal description of a torn and fractured landscape in *Three Essays on the Picturesque* that he had admired:

> The side of a smooth green hill, torn by floods, may at first very properly
> be called deformed, and on the same principle, though not with the same
> impression, as a gash on a living animal. When a rawness of such a gash in the
> ground is softened, and in part concealed and ornamented by the effects of time,
> and the progress of vegetation, deformity, by this usual process, is converted

into picturesqueness; and this is the case with quarries, gravel pits, etc., which at first are deformities, and which in their most picturesque state, are often considered as such by a levelling improver.

So fragments, fissures, and deformities were indeed a legacy of the picturesque.

But time was also a key element of the picturesque, since artists were conscious of recording images of the natural world at a given moment in time: they annotated their sketches with a date and even the hour of the day; weather became (for the first time in the eighteenth century) a major subject matter for the picturesque, and this habit persisted—the American painter John La Farge entitled a painting in the Boston Museum of Fine Arts, *Autumn: October, Noonday, Glen Cove, Long Island, 1860.*

Yet Claude Lorrain said they did that earlier in the seventeenth century— Poussin did "seasons," Dutch and Flemish artists painted the village at noon or at dusk. But, Ruskin said, it was different after the eighteenth century: no longer were these subjects generalized—any season, any dusk, any village—but instead people noted precise times and places, the exact hour of an event and its exact circumstances: hence his admiration for the Pre-Raphaelites (some of them) and for Turner, who would attend to the precise hour and the precise activity that he was depicting. Turner knew that ships in his paintings were doing something specific at a given moment—"going about," "making way," jettisoning cargo.

Nobody at that point raised the whole issue of modern wastelands, toxic or brownfield sites and other cultural deformities. Yet a delight in merely formal effects was generally deemed a liability, though Christopher Tunnard liked the idea that the eighteenth-century picturesque could provide an antidote to the bland and empty gardens and landscapes of the nineteenth century, and he had hoped in the second edition of his book *Gardens in the Modern Landscape* of 1948 to find in the picturesque "a medium for the indulgence of the wildest, irrational caprice" and that, perhaps with modern materials and sculpture, the modern garden would be reborn "as in the Oriental landscape garden and the early Picturesque." Pevsner, once reviled by Basil Taylor in the *Architectural Review* for sponsoring a "Picturesque revival," also argued that a good proportion of accidental and disorderly elements (he called them "varied" and "irregular") lay at the basis even of modernism's success, and he pointed to many architectural moves that played with materials and the planning of buildings and urban landscapes. But he also wanted more than the "absurdity" of pure formalism, which had got the picturesque into so much trouble.

Bois, too, wanted to make more of the picturesque than roughness of medium or even of subject matter. He took up Smithson's challenging remark that the sculptural work of Richard Serra was "picturesque," a notion that Serra himself much resented. Drawing further on both Serra and Smithson, Bois sought to defend Serra's work from a negative understanding of the "picturesque," insisting that the picturesque was a question not of "creating a picture" but of responding to movement on and through "real land"; it was, he said, "an inner movement of the mind" (Ruskin protested this, but Bois went on . . .). If you can manage to reject the picturesque as the flat plane of photograph or canvas, what Serra thought a merely "Gestalt reading," or if in gardening terms you can refuse to see the landscape simply as a view seen from the house, or even if you search for places where such a static and framed view can be taken, then you have properly emancipated yourself from a reductive picturesque. The "true" or "original" picturesque was a struggle against the reduction of "all terrains to the flatness of a sheet of paper," said Bois, quoting René-Louis de Girardin, the creator of eighteenth-century gardens at Ermenonville. Bois also invoked other eighteenth-century proponents of the experience of walking, using the modern writing of Peter Collins on *parallaxis*, a term from the Greek that described a "displacement of the apparent position of a body, due to a change of position of the observer." This could occur in moving toward or past a building or distancing oneself from it, or when perambulating along a line of regular trees set against an arcade in a garden setting (notionally a so-called formal landscape), when the visitor experienced a variety of perspectives due to the combination of objects as he or she passed beside them. Thus the picturesque, properly appreciated, was not something that could be fixed in an image (sketch, photograph); it was to be experienced.

So the eighteenth century saw an expanded picturesque rather than a simple celebration of static pictures in the landscape. So the much touted theorist of the picturesque, Uvedale Price, as Smithson noted, "tried to free landscaping from the picture gardens of Italy," and Smithson therefore saw him as one who had "extended" landscaping from a mere reliance on the picturesque by a celebration of movement. That was all right for some, but Lorrain, who did know the seventeenth century at first hand, objected that strolling was as much a part of the experience of the Villa Lante or Versailles, as well as his and others' exploration of the Roman countryside. But that, said Bois, was why he claimed Capability Brown as picturesque, because Brown valued "deambulatory space and peripatetic vision" (Serra's phrase), even though there was little "picturesque" to be found in Brown's own landscape designs. Ruskin, having been educated with his family's travels through England and Europe, noted that William Gilpin became the picturesque tourist par excellence precisely because he relished movement—though perhaps through the windows of a moving carriage (as the young Ruskin had done with his parents); yet as a young man Gilpin had also *narrated* a long and detailed *stroll* through the gardens of Stowe in a *Dialogue* between two visitors, published in 1748.

Bois's use of Serra's sculpture provided, everyone agreed, a clever and moving defense of the "picturesque." And Serra's hostility to architecture made the relevance to landscape architecture more apt. A Serra piece like the *Clara-Clara*, two tilting arcs for which a ground plan, showing where they rested on the ground, would be meaningless, for it would show neither the tilt of nor the experience of navigating between these two steel arcs. It was a landscape more than a building or even a conventional sculpture; it yielded forms that were "ambiguous, indeterminate, unknown as an entity," as one moved through and around them. Further, though it took Pevsner to make this point in writing of an urban picturesque, the location of *Clara-Clara* in an metropolitan landscape like Paris (which is what Bois illustrated) also transformed how we registered that larger context, letting us respond to the Parisian setting or "landscape" with its "partial and uncertain concealment" (citing Price again) that excites our curiosity. Even Frank Gehry's architecture, *pace* Serra, was another example of how a ground plan was meaningless when compared with our perambulation and exploration of it.

So most agreed that mere forms by themselves and certainly picture making and ground plans were a diminution of the picturesque. Claude Lorrain said that almost all his paintings were not a merely pleasing formal play with shapes and colors, as was claimed later by picturesque gardeners in England, but were focused on narratives of mythological or biblical subjects (Ovid was a favorite source) set within significant landscapes, and the concordance of setting and human action was essential. In his day it was history or narrative paintings, not the mere and minor genre of landscape *tout pur*, that was valued; the viewer, therefore, "moved" through the landscape to grasp its narrative. Ruskin's admiration for Turner was always (or almost always) focused on his attention to the activity of humans within the selected scenery. But then, Lorrain was asked, how do you translate such "speaking pictures," with their focus upon human action, into the built forms of landscape architecture? And this was how the second early aspect of the picturesque was introduced.

The best attempt to describe how pictures could become landscape was to be found in remarks by Joseph Addison and Alexander Pope, remarks that Pevsner recorded when reviewing the early literature of the picturesque. Pope used the term "picturesque" on several occasions to refer to how he imagined characters in Homer's epics would behave; in his commentary on his translations in the 1710s and 1720s he accepts as a matter of course that some human action, some human event, has always to be at the center of any painting and that it is how that person or persons are depicted that can signal how we read or respond to Homer's "paintings." So he asks his readers to picture, among the people in Homer's description of the Trojans burning the Greek ships, the figure of Patroclus, of whom he writes that "nothing could be more natural and affecting than the speech of Patroclus, so nothing is more lively and Picturesque than the attitude he is described in."

Innumerable accounts of landscape visitors in the eighteenth century showed them in "attitudes," either verbally described or graphically represented. Pope's own friend William Kent, who worked for the stage as well as for landscape design and would have known well how actors performed and gestured on the stage, always showed people responding to his proposed landscapes in his sketches: they point, they gesture while apparently moving, they discuss and even (once) have words appended to drawings that suggest what forms such remarks might take. Everywhere in eighteenth-century engravings or landscapes you see people responding, for that is the true and central picturesque "moment": in a painting that Pieter Andreas Rysbrack made of the Orange Tree Garden at Chiswick in the late 1720s (in the Trustees of the Chatsworth Collection), he shows a party emerging through the outer hedges, one of them gesturing to what the group will see once they enter the garden. Kent's role as garden designer was precisely to organize items in the gardens that occasioned this discussion and human activity. So Kent's role at Stowe, in Buckinghamshire, was to design and erect temples dedicated to the Ancients, to British Worthies and to Friendship, and other architects, such as James Gibbs, did the same, providing (since Gibbs was otherwise a determined classicist) a unique Gothic building—called the Temple of Liberty, in front of which visitors would have meditated and conversed upon the role of England's Gothic past.

Tunnard, who should have been a help here, having insisted in his survey of English gardening practice on the variety of items that were used to dot a landscape, missed the real point. For items in the landscape, whether designed or simply found there, were the prompts and triggers by which visitors would respond. That was the true human action within picturesque landscape, both painted and on the ground. In fact, as Ruskin pointed out, the term "landscape architecture" was used, at least till the early nineteenth century, precisely to refer to depictions of architecture in landscape paintings; only later did it come to refer to the making of garden landscapes themselves. Thus buildings, follies, ruins, or even geological happenstance were the means by which humans found their proper role in responding to a designed site.

The other writer whom Pevsner found in the roll call of early picturesque writers was Joseph Addison. In his *Spectator* essay number 414 (1712) Addison enthused about how a landowner might lay out his own property, for which he invoked the Dutch term "landschap" (Englished as landskip, which would eventually become the English term, landscape) to mean how a painter would "represent a view, prospect or opening of a country." Thus he wrote that "Fields of corn make a pleasant Prospect, and if the Walks were a little taken care of that lie between them, if the natural Embroidery of the Meadows were helpt and improved by some Additions of Art, and the several Rows of Hedges set off by Trees and Flowers . . . a Man might make a pretty Landskip of his own possessions." Here the controlling idea is that the "significance" of such a landscape was that it exemplified a person, his station in life; you read the man (usually a man) through what the place or estate told you about that person. His presence, even if not visible in the painting, was the meaning of the painting; it was his "portrait."

That also explains what may seem an odd example by Pope, when he declared, "All gardening is landscape painting. Just like a landscape hung up" and noted that this is done in gardening as in painting: "You may distance things by darkening them and by narrowing the plantation more and more towards the end, in the same manner as they do in painting." The remark is odd, because it was apparently made when Pope was visiting the Botanical Garden in Oxford; nothing strikes us as "picturesque" about it or its landscape; furthermore, there were no figures or human action that he mentions that might have been adduced as central to a painting. Yet if you think of this place itself, of Pope's movement through its seventeenth-century gateway and of its activity of humans studying and responding to the details of the natural world, and think that the Botanical Garden could be viewed down the length of the botanical garden as if distanced by a painter, then it is plausibly picturesque.

But some objected that, though this was all right historically, if you did sufficient archaeology of the term "picturesque" and its uses at that particular period, it had anyway completely lost its way since then. It has no hold now upon how we think of the picturesque. It was useless in any modern context, which was clearly why Richard Serra thought it was an empty, mindless word. Something like a rearguard action took place, however, and the debate returned to a point that Bois had already launched. What was needed, beyond his elegant and informed historical application to the contemporary work of Serra, was to recognize that the picturesque could enjoy a modern role, even if the word itself had been struck by lightning. Even the word itself could be saved.

The "picturesque" had been inserted by late eighteenth-century picturesque theorists into the gap between the sublime and the beautiful, as identified by Edmund Burke in his 1757 book *A Philosophical Enquiry into Our Ideas of the Sublime and Beautiful*. Many saw as the virtue of the picturesque that it partook of both extremes—either the more sublime, private affects or the social world of the beautiful. It broadened the somewhat rigid boundaries that Burke established. Ruskin saw this potential, when in "The Lamp of Memory" he moved to reinstate the "loose" picturesque as what he termed a "Parasitical [or 'engrafted'] Sublimity." He relocated the picturesque closer to the sublime than to the beautiful, mainly because he needed to remove it from being merely a question of "universal decay" and to allow it a "voicefulness" in the articulation of how humans responded to their surroundings. Ruskin certainly acknowledged that "angular and broken lines, vigorous oppositions of light and shadow, and grave, deep, or boldly contrasted colour"—all part of the early notion of *pittoresk* work that Pevsner, too, would admire—are "in a higher degree effective when, by resemblance or association, they remind us of objects on which a true and essentially sublimity exists." These "objects" may be human figures, as in Michelangelo, or objects like buildings or landscape that "admit of a richness of record altogether unlimited," that tell a story or record a fact that directly impacts human responses or action. The power of architecture and landscape, then, is the power of how they affect and infect human action and speak to us.

Ruskin's defense of the picturesque was hedged about with his own idiosyncratic and quasi-religious explanations, and by his anxiety about how much it had become clichéd and devalued in the mid-nineteenth century. Yet Ruskin clearly sensed that the lamp of memory gave to the true picturesque a language of association. He also wished to relieve the word of its solipsistic, altogether private, and random frequency: he needed to return to what he called "a fixed and undoubted criterion, deduced from demonstrable principles and indisputable laws" (citing here his very eighteenth-century belief in socially and commonly held ideas, as explained originally in his essays for the *Architectural Review* of 1838). Pevsner, too, wanted to rely more on agreed and concrete criteria and not just on a modish sensibility.

But Smithson simply bypassed the issue of solipsism, moving the debate to the real possibilities of the modern. He was happy enough to use the word "picturesque" when talking of Richard Serra, but his own "performance" as a picturesque tourist is clear when he visited Passaic in New Jersey. He took with him a camera (his "Instamatic"—what "rationalists call a camera"), and he used this as many eighteenth-century artists used the "Claude glass."

Claude Lorrain interrupted to say he had *never* used this mirror. But certainly Gainsborough showed an artist using this later in the eighteenth century, and furthermore someone offered the fact that "Claude glasses" (square ones in the same shape and the same size as a bill-fold) were still on sale in Philadelphia at the end of the nineteenth century; also on sale were a set of different-colored lenses by which the view to be studied could be tinted to give the desired Claudean effect. More protests from Lorrain. . . .

But Smithson was saying that he used the camera not in the positivist way (like "rationalists") but to capture the detritus, waste lots, and urban debris of Passaic, to record sandboxes, industrial pipes like gushing fountains, and car lots that dot this worn and clapped-out landscape. He quoted Nabokov: "Today our unsophisticated cameras record in their own way our hastily assembled and painted world." For the "rationalist," these were presumably the detritus of "vast, wasted or wasteful land surfaces," what by 2006 Alan Berger was celebrating in his book *Drosscape: Wasting Land in Urban*

America. For Smithson and his alert camera they were, however, "ruins in reverse"—to which he responded by associating these industrial leftovers with "monuments"; yet at the same time, he mocked any pretentious discovery of extravagant sexual meanings in the place, refusing "crass anthropomorphic" explanations of places. It was enough for him to conclude, bringing himself and Passaic together picturesquely, "I will merely say, 'It was there.'" And, as he did later in Central Park, he walked, he explored the real ground. He showed the "dialectic of walking and looking," a central argument of his essay "Frederick Law Olmsted and the Dialectical Landscape," along with a host of other dialectic observations, such as the opposition of the sublime and the beautiful, or places and words, art and nature.

The return of the human meaning or presence can enable or redetermine the "picturesque," and even the huge disturbances of land that today we rediscover in drosscapes, toxic landscapes, and the lacunae of human-induced and human-produced wasteland, that may yield themselves once again to a new generation of landscape architects as a means of understanding an extended picturesque. Clearly the modern picturesque could not (for the moment?) cope with industrial leftovers. Nobody wanted to go there. Instead, it was "the architectural concept of 'promenade'" invented (maybe) by Le Corbusier, according to Bois, that sustained the discussion by the end. And Pevsner, not only anthologizing early writing about the picturesque, also amassed a portfolio of images, which his editor would posthumously set out as *Visual Planning and the Picturesque.* These photographs are all, of course, "static," and people did object to "the reduction of all terrains to the flatness of a sheet of paper" (Serra again), and say that "the ability to make picturesque sketches [in this case photographs] was a fatal gift to the architect"—an aside there, from Adrian Forty, the author of *Forty Words and Buildings: A Vocabulary of Modern Architecture* (2004). But Pevsner's photographs are glossed particularly with his account of "sequences," of the "roving eye" (he hints at the old tradition of parallax), his fascination with gateways, thresholds, and entrances, "a few steps down" as we are "led" into an Oxford quadrangle, momentary sightings, surprises down high streets and lanes, turns to right and left, contractions in new spaces after leaving expansive openings. It was a visual and verbal celebration of the "multiplicity of views" (Serra again), recalling the whole business of gardeners like Humphry Repton who "survey the scene while in motion." But it was not simply a free grouping and mixture of materials, nor a play with forms, nor, of course, with Pevsner, a nostalgic trip down the memory lanes of Oxford and the Inns of Court (that would be the forte of his contemporary, John Betjeman). Mies van der Rohe's Barcelona Pavilion, admired by Tunnard, and Corbu's "intriguing and most enchanting variety of vistas in all directions" (cited by Pevsner) were as much at the heart of this mobile and modern picturesque as was the simple confection of old buildings by Inigo Jones, Gilbert Scott, and Robert Taylor that were visible in Pevsner's photographs.

So could there be a future for the picturesque? It was an essential aspect of modernism, the watershed of which, Bois pointed out, was in the later eighteenth century, after the advent of Hume, the "forefather of modern phenomenology." Everybody said yes, but nobody wanted to live with the tired old word. Nobody wanted to see "pictures," or to use the viewfinder of a camera, let alone a Claude glass; even with the movie camera or video, you were pinned to the eyehole (like, nobody wanted to walk *and* chew gum). Nobody appreciated the crazy idea of a national park in New Zealand that had actually set up huge picture frames around the place, so that visitors could capture [*sic*] the landscape through them. But the idea that we observed while walking, that places changed as we maneuvered around or past them, that there was movement of the mind largely because there was movement of the feet, these were not only useful but essential human activities. The picturesque promoted (Bois citing Price again) "partial and uncertain concealment" that "excites and nourishes curiosity." So there was good reason to trim the lamp of memory and furnish the mind with associations and ideas, wherever those might be found in a varied and fractured world, and the discussion came to an end. Drinks all round, and the landscape architects picked up the tab.

Chapter 6

Folly in the Garden

The folly came to be an essential element in landscapes during the eighteenth and nineteenth centuries and has generally been seen ever since as a whimsical or frivolous move in design. But as follies were apt as triggers and prompts for responding to sites, so their use continues as a means whereby designers can promote reactions in their visitors.

I am not ignorant what an ill report Folly hath got, even amongst the most Foolish.
—Erasmus, *In Praise of Folly*

THERE HAS, OF COURSE, been much foolishness in gardens from the very beginning. And after foolishly earning their banishment from Eden, humans have more often than not explained their establishment of new gardens as a "re-creation" of that lost paradise. The bravado of such gestures—whether large (Versailles) or small (the makeover of your or my backyard)—may perpetuate the original foolishness; for if one considers the inevitable fragility and the built-in entropy of all gardens, let alone the precariousness of taste, it seems a great folly even to start one. Yet while garden making might indeed be a great folly, it can also be—in the tradition of Erasmus's famous reflections—a wonderful foolishness near allied to genius or wisdom. It is not, however, so much the large folly of garden-making that concerns me here as the local or particular folly in the garden. This architectural insertion is, of course, a subtheme of the larger folly, in that it introduces within a garden a piece of work that can be by turns silly, vain, trivial, foolish, and fragile (on the one hand) and (on the other) an inspired invention, a magical open sesame to a permanent world of imaginative scenery.

The National Trust in Britain is the custodian of innumerable follies; so reasonably enough it published in 1986 a gazetteer of British examples, *Follies: A Guide,* in which the two authors (Gwyn Headley and Wim Meulenkamp) included among the sites of their gazetteer Apollo's Temple in Ian Hamilton Finlay's garden at Little Sparta at Dunsyre in Scotland (Figure 27). Finlay was outraged at the whole enterprise, and he pilloried the authors in various publications from his Wild Hawthorne Press and by the so-called Committee of Public Safety at Little Sparta. It may help us to begin an inquiry into the garden and landscape folly to ask why Finlay was, justifiably in my view, goaded into protest, and into his antagonism directed at the authors' meager estimate of the folly as an architectural item.

The authors' introduction begins with "Ideally, [a folly] should be a big, Gothick, ostentatious, over-ambitious and useless structure, probably with a wildly improbable local legend attached" (p. xxi). The authors then demur (unconvincingly) about their own categorization, asserting that in fact the folly defies "even such broad definitions"; they end their initial paragraph with "The folly must lie in the eye of the beholder," to which the retort might well be, "precisely."[1] The only thing these two authors even begin to get right is the emphasis, such as it is, on "locality." Otherwise, their lightweight notion of this by now traditional garden element simply does not grapple with a fundamental ambition of all garden or landscape follies, namely, that they are there to prompt some serious, though not necessarily solemn, meditation upon the site where the folly is discovered, which it enhances by enlarging a visitor's experience of that particular place. Such an ambition has, not surprisingly, often been hard to fulfill, which is where foolishness has entered the folly. But at its most strenuous and successful the garden or landscape folly is a built or material form of the rhetorical strategy of *prosopopeia.*

Prosopopeia is the device by which a poet or orator imagines something in the landscape speaking directly to a privileged visitor or passerby.[2] A famous biblical example is when Moses is told by a voice from heaven, "Put

27. Ian Hamilton Finlay, Apollo's Temple. Little Sparta. Photograph by Emily T. Cooperman.

thy shoes from off thy feet, for the place whereon thou standst is holy ground." Other versions involve a physical item, sometimes incorporating an inscription, which—though it must have been deliberately placed in the landscape— can somehow be imagined as self-generating and speaking through itself on behalf of the place where it is inserted and encountered. Graveyards, burial places, and memorials have always been privileged in this respect, because they may house the remains of famous people who thereby give a particular resonance or meaning to the site and because their final resting places are usually marked in some way that invariably includes inscriptions.[3] Thomas Gray's "Elegy" is a prime example of a poet seized by what he reads on the

28. Thomas Gainsborough, "Wooded Landscape with Peasant Reading Tombstone, Rustic Lovers and Ruined Church," 1779–80, reprinted 1797. © Tate, London 2015.

gravestones in the country churchyard, and what is arguably Gainsborough's illustration of Gray depicts an anonymous country man bending down to decipher a gravestone where some inscription (as we would now say) "speaks to him" (Figure 28).

Other pictorial versions of this prosopopeia are more famous, like Nicolas Poussin's shepherds who stumble upon an inscribed tomb in the pastoral country of Arcadia. The inscription reads, "Et in Arcadia Ego," a resonant phrase that the art historian Erwin Panofsky long ago interpreted as the utterance, not of some person buried in this tomb, but of death itself: "Even I, death, have been [or am] in Arcadia."[4] What is so compelling about these paintings (Poussin executed two versions of this theme) is the drama of the encounter between the young, beautiful citizens of Arcady and the tomb, emblem enough of death and burial; but what is also disturbing is that a pastoral enclave supposedly immune to transience and decay cannot ultimately thwart these youths (Figure 29). A further aspect of these paintings, implied by the various gestures of the young people, is their gradual realization, as they

29. Nicolas Poussin, *Et in Arcadia Ego*, c. 1640, oil on canvas, Musée du Louvre, Paris, France. © RMN-Grand Palais / Art Resource, NY.

begin to decipher the inscription, of the presence of death; not one death, but death in their country of Arcady. The shepherds' epiphany, which we might presume utterly changes their (as it does our) understanding of Arcadian perfection, comes then in a twofold sequence: first the object, the tomb, in the landscape, its architectural and sculptural forms being a mute language that catches the attention of the alert passersby; and then, via its actual inscribed words, initiating a larger comprehension of the significance of where they find themselves. That the tomb speaks in a classical language would be enough in the seventeenth century—along with the shepherd's clothing—to indicate that this dramatic moment takes place in an antique landscape.[5]

HERE IS, then, a prototype of the landscape folly as it would evolve in the eighteenth century: a physical thing from the past that speaks a special message to those who want and who are able to read it. Ian Hamilton Finlay knew this tradition well—he may not have known of the rhetorical term "prosopopeia," but he was versed in the varied use of inscriptions in two of his favorite and much cited eighteenth-century gardens, William Shentone's The Leasowes and the marquis of Girardin's Ermenonville. In his own garden of Little Sparta Finlay explored the implications of using inscriptions in a modern context, of privileged visitors being halted and addressed by something in the landscape that alerted them to more than just its physical shape, context, or conventional meaning. It is part, a major part, of his much vaunted neoclassicism, but a neoclassicism retooled for contemporary purposes.[6]

A scattering of inscriptions in the garden of Little Sparta elaborates that experience. In one, man is acknowledged as a "passerby" (Figure 30), who may be expected stop and stoop to read inscriptions like this one, as did Gray's poet and Gainsborough's peasants; it is in English, like another that laments, "The world has been empty since the Romans," empty of Latin among other things but also—we may infer—empty of any sense of the special meanings of place, for it is drained of the sacred or noumenous, perhaps because the world now lacks a suitable language in which to express it. Another item recalls the gravestones and tombs encountered in Gray and Poussin by both its tombstone shape and the formulation—now in Latin—of its "HIC JACET . . . " (Here lies . . .). The whole inscription (Figure 31) translates, "Here lies a small extract from a larger [piece of] water," an admonition that may remind us how a garden extracts something from the larger world beyond its boundaries: a pond is the epitome of an ocean, for example, but at the same time also a diminishment, a little death. Such inscriptions, detaining the passerby who wishes to read and understand them, are a major device in Finlay's garden and landscape designs; he places them on a variety of architectural and sculptural items—buildings, columns, sundials, tablets, bridges, walls, and on bricks, pebbles, and stones embedded in the ground.

But outside of his garden making Finlay also deployed and reenvisaged Poussin's painting. He and his collaborator Gary Hincks substituted modern emblems of death and destruction to make more emphatic the presence of death and destruction amid a scenery where the average person today would locate only the bland and sentimental world of nature. Poussin could invoke Latin and a Roman sarcophagus; Finlay has to use the German Nazi tank and its SS insignia to force the recognition of the violence of nature (including human nature). This imagery was later revisited in a series of emblems entitled *The Wartime Garden*, drawn by Ron Costley, and its theme was eventually transferred into a series of analogous insertions in the garden of Little Sparta

30. Ian Hamilton Finlay, "Passerby," Little Sparta. Photograph by Emily T. Cooperman.

31. Ian Hamilton Finlay, "Hic Jacet . . . ," Little Sparta. Photograph by Emily T. Cooperman.

itself. Their ironic playfulness—a German warning about mines concealed in the ground is simply the site where the underground electricity cable enters the property, aircraft carriers are miniaturized into bird tables—sometimes masks the seriousness, the intensity of Finlay's reminder that warfare and violence are an ineluctable part of nature; the humor may even serve to make the admonition more compelling, though it can also encourage the passerby to dismiss it. Something nasty in the shrubbery, nonetheless.

We can now return to the National Trust book of follies that so affronted Finlay. Though it mentions briefly his own garden temple, where inscriptions hail Apollo for his missiles as well as his music and his muses, and it is extremely patronizing if not scornful about the inscriptions throughout the site,[7] what Finlay in fact reacted to was Headley and Meulenkamp's total disregard of both the traditions of garden insertions that "spoke" to visitors and, more precisely, the role of these insertions in declaring the particular meaning of a place, in short, their disregard of the tradition and idea of genius loci. The phrase is of course at once resonant and somewhat tired, yet also resilient, in that no alternative phrase has intervened to do its work adequately.

THE CLASSICAL tradition of genius loci has—as far as we are concerned—three aspects: that a place was sacred because it was peopled by deities; that these deities represented the specific character of a place; and that it behooved visitors to recognize and respect the particular site so identified and protected by its guardian spirits. It comprised both a belief in spirits and divinities and an understanding that every place was unique and special, if properly perceived. The second emphasis could and did survive even when the first—the polytheism—was discarded or lost sight of. William Blake famously recounted that loss of spiritual faith in his *Marriage of Heaven and Hell*: its eleventh plate recalls how the "enlarged & numerous senses" of ancient poets *animated* everything they encountered, placing each city and county "under its mental deity," until modern rationalism and religion abstracted and systemized this ancient responsiveness to place. Despite Blake's particular skepticism, the idea of and even belief in genius loci has not entirely succumbed to rationalist or Gradgrindian positivism. The modern philosopher and landscape critic André Roger may well insist that "en lui-même, le génie du lieu n'existe pas," but he sneaks it back in as merely a cultural construction, jettisoning any supernaturalism and making fun in the process of somebody like Maurice Barrès, who in his *La colline inspirée* of 1912 wrote of "des lieux où souffle l'esprit . . . qui tirent l'âme de sa léthargie, des lieux enveloppés, baignés de mystère, élus de toute éternité pour être le siège de l'émotion religieuse" (places breathe the spirit . . . that draw the soul from its lethargy, places enveloped, bathed in mystery, elected through eternity to be the seat of a religious feeling).[8] But anyone who recalls E. M. Forster's short story "The Road from Colonus" will surely understand what Barrès, for all his incantatory prose, was getting at: that places do reach out and seize one with an emotion that is—Blake would happily acknowledge—spiritual without being religious. And Hegel, too, invoked this same understanding of noumena by explaining how the "ancient Greek . . . demanded the meaning of springs, mountains, forests, storms; without knowing what all these objects said to him one by one, he perceived in the order of the vegetable world and of the cosmos an immense *frisson* of meaning, to which he gave the name of a god, Pan."[9] Some faint intimation of this understanding undoubtedly explains why in some eighteenth-century gardens Pan can still haunt the shrubbery in sculptural guise.

But by the time a Pan figure was inserted into the glades and groves of the gardens at Rousham, Oxfordshire, in the late 1730s, classical notions of genius loci had already begun to be profoundly modified. We can track this in Alexander Pope's use of the phrase in his instructions to the landscaper in his 1731 *Epistle to Burlington*. "Consult the genius of the place in all," he wrote; but when we listen to what that genius actually is or does, it turns out to be the topography itself—the hills, vales, glades, woods—rather than any immanent spirit, which is supplied in fact not by some in-dwelling deity but by the landscape designer, who, attentive to those physical elements, makes of them something else—ambitious hills, circling vales, opening glades, and willing woods. The genius of the place elicits the imagination or genius of the good designer: it takes one to know one. Pope's intuition, then, is of an objective place transformed by the intervention of a respectful subject, whose primary skill is an understanding of topography. Though Pope certainly knew and loved landscapes where the designer had done more than just manipulate the natural terrain, his public instructions at this point make no proposals for insertions like Pan statues, Apollonian temples, or inscriptions. The genius of place apparently must speak for itself.

Finlay situates his garden work within those eighteenth-century traditions—he shares Pope's view that the genius of a designer can elicit and manifest the particular character or significance of a place; yet, because presumably he thinks we have lost the understanding and appreciation of that subtle demonstration, he also needs to augment it with insertions of statues, inscriptions, and temples (if not of Pan, at least with references to Pan's home ground, Arcady). And for this he has recourse to other eighteenth-century gardenists like Shenstone and Girardin. He insists upon the sacredness of place, not because he still believes in the deities who reside in trees and streams and meadows, but because places continue—or must continue to be, or can be made to be special, numinous, and not debased in a merely secular culture. (It is important to register that Finlay's denunciation of the secular runs throughout his writings). So when Finlay denounced the book by Headley and Meulenkamp it was because they utterly failed to understand that follies were one of many—but also a prime—agent by which the noumenous or nonsecular aspect of genius loci might be revived. He wrote to me at the time specifically to protest the "hideous process of secularization" perpetrated by the National Trust book; to another correspondent he lamented the Trust's inability to do what it was supposed to do, "conserve traditions,"[10] among which presumably was that of genius loci.

Now Finlay's own response to genius loci was to return to some exemplary eighteenth-century gardens. In these, patrons and designers tried to address the specifically modern question of how, given a recognition of some special quality or meaning in a place but without recourse to "mental deities," you represent genius loci in practice and on the ground. There were dozens of ways in which this was attempted, depending upon what aspect of place was in question. Places and their "genius" could be local, regional, national. Places could draw out connections with contemporaries—celebrating the living owner—or with dead-and-gone inhabitants. These insertions into the landscape of an estate—tombs, ruins, temples, pavilions, columns, statuary, or inscriptions—certainly enhanced the spatiality of a site by orientating the visitor, leading his or her eye and feet to explore the place more thoroughly. But they could also enhance its temporality, situating its particular moment in histories that, once again, could be recent and local or distant and sublimely global in scope. The essentially atavistic or memorializing mode of this genius loci (for a place could not easily commemorate a future event or person) explains the obvious choice of a tomb or gravestone as the marker of choice: thus C. Gay's *prix d'émulation* design for a cenotaph for Sir Isaac Newton in 1800 was intended for a park setting, maybe even the Folie Sainte-James.[11] The opportunities for such utterances of history and geography were vast, not to say sublime, and the difficulty of employing them convincingly goes a long way to explain the bathetic and foolish uses of the folly that gave this landscape architectural vocabulary a bad name. So much of a bad name, that Bernard Tschumi's grid of red follies in Parc de la Villette in Paris has seemed to some critics the final absurdity of this mode, the empty invocation by an architect who didn't adequately know his landscape history, or who perhaps did, hence his deliberately empty gesture (see Figure 35).

That folly, or *folie* in French, became the word and the general means of ascribing and inscribing a sense of place had good etymological reasons. In France the word had been originally used to refer to country retreats shaded by leaves (*foleia* in Latin) and to crude buildings made from tree branches; equally, a Latin root (*foliates*) underlies the English use of folly to refer to a hilltop copse or small woodland without necessarily any structure added to it.[12] These topographical gestures survived even when the modern meaning of foolishness or madness was dominant: in the fifteenth century a wealthy merchant's extravagant country mansion was dubbed "La Folie Regnault," and the name survived on maps of 1675, 1707, and 1728, by when it had passed into the hands of Jesuits, who elaborated the grounds even more (the site eventually became the cemetery of Père Lachaise in the early nineteenth century).[13] The term "folie" continued to serve in France for mansions and gardens the extravagance of which earned a mixture of disapprobation, mockery, and yet awe at the huge gestures by which a landscape was fashioned to stimulate the visitor's imagination and thereby of course to aggrandize its proprietor. Among the most famous sites accorded this label in the later eighteenth century were Bagatelle (La Folie d'Artois), Tivoli (La Folie Boutin), and (by far the best known) La Folie Sainte-James.[14] All these sites were scattered with individual structures that thereby and subsequently also acquired the individual label of folly.

An important historical question is why the device of the folly flourished, and often foolishly failed, in the eighteenth-century landscape? Despite the early usage of the term in France applied to country houses, rudely constructed huts, and grandiose architectural gestures, the extensive use and abuse of architectural and sculptural insertions in a landscape may arguably be located in the early eighteenth century and in England, as a means of activating visitors' imaginations to respond to the place where they were encountered. And it is, I believe, useful to distinguish these inventive supplements from the Renaissance and baroque practice of incorporating iconographical items in an overall garden design (the statue of Hercules at Vaux-le-Vicomte, for example) and above all from the iconographical programs of the sort that Louis XIV and his committees installed and reinstalled in the gardens of Versailles. Such iconographical elements continued to be used, after the Renaissance and even after the baroque, but they gradually lost ground to the newer mode of the folly—though sometimes the folly would rely upon iconographical elements to communicate. An item like the copy of Scheemaker's sculptural group representing a lion attacking a horse that William Kent moved to such a prominent position overlooking the Oxfordshire countryside at Rousham may certainly be given an iconographical gloss—it exactly replicates a similar piece in the Villa d'Este, where it stood for the power struggle between Rome and

32. Rousham, a close-up of the Eye Catcher on the far hillside. Photograph by the author.

Tivoli. But in Rousham, its deliberate placement on the threshold of a larger prospect asked visitors to compare the ineluctably English landscape before them with the Roman *campagna* over which the piece in its Italian site looked, and thereby reflect on cultural displacement and change. The sculptural group has, then, I suggest, moved to perform a moment of prosopopeia more in keeping with what the eighteenth century would later come to term a folly.

Rousham in the 1730s is one among other crucial examples where we can watch the emergence of various forms of the garden or landscape folly as an inherent part of the new landscaping termed "English" or "natural." Early English landscaping insisted, in both its theoretical justifications and built work, upon its indigenous, its native qualities. On the ground, this involved above all invoking the local traditions of sites, recalling local history, local personalities, local architecture; local English architecture meant essentially the Gothic, however shakily understood at that date. At Rousham, Kent deliberately enhanced the local agrarian meaning of the estate by supplementing the local mill with flying buttresses and Gothick battlements; and for his military patron General Dormer he set up a triumphal arch on a facing hillside (Figure 32). But this is hardly what Headley and Meulenkamp term "a straightforward eyecatcher" (p. 264); we associate triumphal arches with ancient Rome, but this is now erected in the Gothic mode because the soldier and his estate it celebrates are English! Earlier and farther north in Yorkshire, Castle Howard had earlier welcomed its visitors through a short line of mock battlements and massive Vanbrugian gateways, to live up to and underline the name of the place and the lineage of a cadet branch of the ancient Howard family. Whig lords like Cobham at Stowe, whose family name was Temple, caused Gothic temples to be added to the landscape like his triangular Temple of Liberty (James Gibbs's only exercise in this style); it was once surrounded by busts of the northern deities who lent their names to the English words for the days of the week.

The examples can be extended, but so far they all involve insertions into landscapes that called up, clarified, or consolidated the significance of a particular place: a significance either political—Gothic liberty at Stowe—or genealogical—junior Howards with their own castle—or merely celebratory of local pieties—as at Rousham. The interest in and fascination with Englishness in all its cultural aspects ensured that gardens and parks were given appropriate items to prompt visitors' associations along those lines. In a long and well-known letter of 1724 Pope described a visit to Sherborne Castle in Dorset, but also how he would improve its landscape. The existing modern house had been built for Sir Walter Raleigh, and there were "several venerable Ruins of an Old Castle," destroyed in the Civil War; so Pope's recommendation to his friend Lord Digby was to "cultivate these ruins and do honour to them . . . [and] sett up at the Entrance of 'em an Obelisk, with an inscription of the Fact: which would be a Monument erected to the very Ruins; as the adorning & beautifying them in the manner I have been imagining, would not be unlike the AEgyptian Finery of bestowing Ornament and curiosity on dead bodies. The Present Master of this place . . . needs not to . . . Shun the Remembrance of the actions of his Forefathers."[15]

Where ancient remains and associations were available and plain to see and read, there was no need to contrive what Horace Walpole called the "true rust of the barons' wars" (he was thinking of the wholly new landscape at Castle Hagley!).[16] Indeed, ancient British remains were often available—like Shenstone's Priory, or Studley Royal's prospect of Fountains Abbey glimpsed from its regular water gardens, and other ruined choirs where late the sweet birds sang. As such they could be augmented, and visitors' attention drawn to their significance. But if they were entirely lacking, suitable inventions were easily designed and accommodated. Painshill has its Gothick tower and an open-sided belvedere—elegant enough but a touch incongruous. Pope's friend Lord Bathurst built King Alfred's Hall in his park at Cirencester between 1721 and 1734 so as to have a "truly" old piece of architecture, but also to declare his alignment with ancient British traditions of liberty that mattered enormously after the Glorious Revolution of 1688. For another landowner, King Alfred also had a special appeal, and Henry Hoare erected Alfred's Tower, decorated with his statue and an inscription lauding his work, on the ridge above Stourhead (see Figure 17). His political gesture was in the same tradition as Bathurst's, but here in Wiltshire Hoare had the extra satisfaction of drawing out the genius loci of an English locality explicitly connected to the figure celebrated. Nonetheless, other Gothic elements that were not so local were brought into the Stourhead landscape: the genuinely medieval Bristol Market Cross, another authentic St. Peter's Pump (see Figure 21), along with stained glass from Glastonbury Abbey, all joined the existing parish church in a declaration of long-established Englishness. And as the eighteenth century grew old, the memory of the early proponents of a truly English landscape were folded into the historical associations: memorials became de rigueur—ones to James Thomson, author of an indispensably English poem *The Seasons,* were incorporated at Stowe and Hagley, seats were dedicated to Pope, also at Hagley, or to Kent at Hackfell. Shenstone, strapped for money to improve The Leasowes in a big way, spent most of his funds on seats and urns dedicated to the presiding genii of his love of landscape. In France, later, the Abbé de Lille who had written his poem celebrating the new garden style was often memorialized and quoted in inscriptions.

But the mention of The Leasowes, with its grove named for Virgil, and more resonantly the example of Stourhead, raises the question, then, why alongside the particularly British elements at Stourhead were at least three classical temples, two of which were derived from authentic classical buildings in Rome and Balbec? Indeed, modern criticism of Stourhead has largely ignored its Gothic elements to concentrate on classical insertions that seem to us these days so much more potent, but also much more readable: they speak something we understand and invoke an iconography readily deciphered. Similarly, Castle Howard has its classicizing Temple of Winds, a Palladian bridge, and a classical mausoleum; Rousham, its classical Praeneste arcade derived from the Temple of Fortune at Palestrina, and so on.

Whatever cultural investments in ancient British history and custom were declared, England could not escape her classical debts, which had also to be brought into play in these landscapes. And these were indeed, insertions, creations *ab nuovo*, for the simple reason that England was less obviously rich in at least visible Roman remains. The Pantheon had to be recreated on a smaller scale at Stourhead, as had the Praeneste Terrace at Rousham. But the presence of both classical and Gothic buildings, two different historical markers, ensured what for many was a vital dialogue between different cultural traditions and their dual contributions to the formation of a resilient Englishness.

BUT THE more intriguing questions are, first, to explain the rapid profusion of landscape insertions that neither had a native British raison d'être nor paid tribute to antecedents in classical culture, and, second, to explain why these devices found such a rapid *succès de folie* across the English Channel.[17]

At Painshill, for example, besides a Gothic pavilion there was a Turkish Tent, lovingly restored at the end of the twentieth century (Figure 33). Stourhead—and this commentators often forget—had a Chinese bridge, a Chinese

33. The restored Turkish Tent, Painshill, Surrey.
Photograph by the author.

umbrella, and a Chinese pavilion, along with a Turkish tent, all now lost. As early as 1738 Stowe added a Chinese house to its compendium of cultural references. Increasingly across England there rose pagodas, Egyptian pyramids (one at Rousham), obelisks, Chinese bridges, and houses of all sorts, sizes, and cultures. The publication of pattern books, devoted to suggesting such fabrications, to be constructed often in cheap and tawdry materials, ensured that the taste for them spread rapidly. The sheer proliferation of folly types, so many of which could never be justified or explained as declaring some genius of a place either English or anywhere else in Europe, meant that they ceased to be used or understood as having any links to locality and meaningful place. At their best, they were fun, scenographic, and colorful, which is why the craze for these decorations could so easily be exported to other European countries.

Pattern books constituted a minor publishing genre, and the fashion spread quickly across Europe, as professional designers, enlightened amateurs, along with the Squire Mushrooms, or later Bouvards and Pécuchets, anyone (in short) who wanted to decorate their gardens by latching on to the latest fad, all found nourishment in the eclectic designs that these books contained. The range is baffling: from Johann Bernard Fischer von Erlach's *Entwurff einer historischen Architektur,* published in Vienna in 1721, one of the earliest texts to parade Eastern items, to Krafft and Dubois's 1809 two-volume *Productions de plusieurs architectes . . . relatives aux jardins pittoresques et aux fabriques de divers genres qui peuvent entrer dans leur composition*. The title says it clearly: these items are an indispensable adjunct to any picturesque garden; they are to "enter" or be inserted into any composition as so much *staffage* and decoration. There is no need to justify them by any substantial cultural reference or local enhancement of place. Temples were available in classical, Turkish, or Egyptian styles; boats and bridges in Egyptian and Chinese; a bowling alley was in the Persian mode, along with Tyrolean mills and Moorish tombs and gateways. But the vernacular modes were also entertained: a man who dressed the vineyard could be housed in a lodging shaped like a huge wine barrel, and a hunting lodge built in the classical style could be dedicated to the huntress Diana.

Doubtless, there could be an occasional propriety in style or dedication; some structures doubtless justified their location and meaning—the bridge and Chinese house (originally white and blue) erected in 1747 at Shugborough in England for Thomas Anson was taken from sketches by a naval officer serving in the Far East with Admiral Anson, Thomas's brother. Nor, of course, can we be sure that landowners who relied on pattern books for ideas did not select something apt for their situation, something that might enhance their particular locality, but that we do not recognize. When a quotation from the Abbé de Lille was carved on a giant rock at Morfortaine, we have no way of knowing how it affected the passersby who stopped to read it and whether it enhanced their understanding of where they were. But essentially the rise and fall of the folly, its spread and dilution, were due to more and more people, many of whom had no tradition of landownership, wanting to create landscapes and gardens that in their turn needed to be turned out in the best modern taste. The pattern books made clear, however, that a touch of Chinese or any other cultural style of *fabrique* could enliven the spare green world of the so-called English landscaping style, which by the second half of the eighteenth century was thought by many to be boring, dull, "differing very little from common fields," and so ready and even willing to be enlivened with a variety of exotic structures.[18]

I WANT, however, to guard against a wholesale, snobbish dismissal of fabriques and follies for being empty and shallow, as flimsy as some of their lathe and canvas materials actually were. Design as scenography has a bad name in current landscape architecture, and the fabrications devised by the pattern books and their incidence throughout late eighteenth-century Europe often seem (as they of course were in many cases) merely a theatrical backdrop for weak social fantasies. But if the folly in its various forms was a way of signaling a special understanding of place, then its continued if weakened invocation may have something still to do with a lingering appreciation of genius loci. The appeal of the folly to the Bouvards and Péchucets of the world, to the nouveau riche and upstart bankers like M. de Sainte-James, was that they needed to feel established, rooted, grounded in a place. Aristocrats and landed gentry were by their very birth and social situation able to see themselves as belonging, owing their station to their residence in a specific place, in a territory the space of which had also a temporal—often a long— history. The (re-)presentation of this inherited status through the elaboration and design of estate grounds was part of their obligation and their privilege, and the cult of the folly was a carefully contrived vocabulary by which a place spoke for its owners and to its visitors.

Moreover, the landscape and its carefully inserted fabriques could be re-invented for other serious purposes as well as for frivolous self-promotion. A cluster of sites in prerevolutionary France reveals how rich was the potential of the folly as a language of both political and cultural commentary, even as it could also betray itself as a gratuitous and superficial plaything. At Ermenonville the marquis de Girardin created scenes in the manner of different painters and with inscriptions that referenced a cluster of writers from Theocritus to Gessner and Rousseau. But his political beliefs drove much of these installations: a Temple of Modern Philosophy, left incomplete with columns lying on the ground to be erected when philosophy had extended its scope, is unique among follies in calling attention to the future, not the past, of a site; no less prospective and modern is the modest, vernacular cabin built for Jean-Jacques Rousseau to inhabit in the wilderness, even if, after the philosopher's death at Ermenonville, the landscape turned elegiac with his tomb, designed by Hubert Robert and installed on the island of poplars. But Girardin used other insertions—the Prairie Arcadienne, the Liberty Tree, archery butts where local people could practice, examples of primitive architecture, prehistoric burial chambers, as well as memorials of Rousseau—to make of his estate a place where the peasants were well regarded and educated and where a propitious sociopolitical future could be projected.

34. The Ruined Column, Désert de Retz.
Photograph by the author.

At the Désert de Retz, incidentally included by Headley and Meulen-kamp among their "finest, purest foll[ies] in the world" (p. xxviii), M. de Monville arguably organized his retreat after 1774 to invoke a cluster of historical and cultural references: twenty items were devised and inserted, including a Chinese Pavilion built of teak, a pyramid (doubling as an ice house), a Temple of Pan, a Gothic church (a genuine ruin), a Turkish tent, and the Broken Column (Figure 34). The truncated enormity of this last feature suggested that long ago the parkland was inhabited by a race of stupendous beings; indeed, the Scotsman Thomas Blaikie was put in mind of the Tower of Babel. Lovingly restored in recent years, the Désert de Retz is still a place of mysteries, "at the antipodes of ordinary life";[19] it recalls cultures that haunt our consciousness, yet remains emphatically modern in its determination to characterize this particular place and time by a celebration of one man's wish to transcend them all.

That broken column is at once a colossal absurdity and visionary poetry, and no wonder it has attracted a similar range of enthusiasts, from Thomas Jefferson, André Breton, and the surrealists to Yves Bonnefoy. It is less certain whether a slightly earlier creation, the Jardin Monceau, the remains of which

Chapter 6

have become a public park in the eighth arrondissement of Paris, was able to blend lively frivolity with a serious meditation upon "all times and all places" in the same fashion as the Désert de Retz. That was at least the claim of its designer, Carmontelle, in his publication on the site. He put his previous theatrical and festival-making skills at the service of the duc de Chartres, and laid out a bewildering assemblage of sceneries all focused on suitable structures—Dutch, Turkish, Chinese, Egyptian, ancient Roman (the Naumachia still survives, but not the Temple of Mars), cheek by jowl with agricultural farms, vineyards, and a chemical laboratory that led into greenhouses. The whole was so astonishing, ambiguous in its mixture of frivolity and zeal, that the need to claim it as a site designed for Masonic rituals has been irresistible (a similar claim for the Désert de Retz is far less convincing). Whatever subtext is plausible, the effort of the whole was to invent a genius loci to outdo any merely local and historical understanding of the site. Today Parc Monceau observes, if at all, a different sense of place: well-to-do Parisians walk their dogs and their children, amid a few relics of prerevolutionary fantasy, in a green space reinvented for them by Baron Haussmann in the nineteenth century.

A fourth late eighteenth-century example also challenges our tolerance for and historical understanding of its extraordinary inventions. The Folie of the extremely rich businessman Claude Bernard de Sainte-James was the work of François-Joseph Bélanger, to whom his patron in the late 1780s gave carte blanche to outdo earlier folies, including the architect's own previous remodeling of Bagatelle. The resulting series of fabriques, many copied from earlier French sites, are whimsically recorded on seventeen buttons painted by Louis Bélanger and preserved in a velvet case; on the ground their prolixity was dazzling (it would be "very beautiful," said one visitor, "if there was less of it").[20] Visitors were confronted with an eclectic series of sceneries, admonitions, and prompts to their imagination: Bacchus, Cupid, and Psyche vied with the sphinx, a vast cabinet of natural history, artificial rocks, a steam pump, columns, kiosks, and trellis-work pavilions. What remains today has perhaps a more authentic sense of place, an aptly fragmented tribute to the French indulgence in follies,[21] which does suggest that folly matured is wisdom gained. But in the face of the Folie Sainte-James, it was no wonder that the English wanted to distance themselves from the extent and excess of the French deployment of follies in their late eighteenth-century landscapes, for which, they guiltily realized, they were in large part responsible: "The Lord knows what barbarism is going to be laid at our door," wrote Horace Walpole after a visit in 1771. "The new *Anglomanie* will literally be *mad English*."[22]

FOOLISHNESS, as we know, is never-ending, and the fun of folly doesn't go away. So it is no surprise that modern architecture has played with the revival of the folly. Garden festivals have witnessed a resurgence of the folly, its invention doubtless sustained by the knowledge that its life on such sites is short and the impact needed must be big: for the Dutch biennale Floriade of 1989 a dozen young architects proposed a set of follies, while their publication traced a concise and sympathetic history of the genre.[23] Architects without even the opportunity of a temporary site have enjoyed playing with eccentric forms that evince no palpable usefulness: in 1983 galleries in both New York and Los Angeles hosted an exhibition entitled *Follies; Architecture for the Late Twentieth-Century Landscape*, for which Rizzoli published a catalogue of proposals by nineteen architects and an introductory essay by Anthony Vidler. Vidler championed the folly's now familiar ambiguity ("at best sublime and at worst frivolous" [p. 13]), celebrated its perverse internal logic ("withdrawn from the world . . . in a sense pure"), and argued for its relevance as providing an asylum for "the forbidden, for the repressed, for the denied and the absolutely impossible." That appeal at least undertakes to extend the genre as Freudian follies *de nos jours*. But all the projects were placeless, were not designed for a particular place.[24]

Bernard Tschumi was among those exhibitors in 1983, but the follies he actually got to erect at Parc de la Villette (conceived for the international design competition at the same time as the American exhibitions) are sited in an actual place (Figure 35). The grid of bright red follies, which seems a colorful but empty gesture to many people, strikes me as having a shrewd if ironic motive: the grid is an ideally modern form since it can be established and extended, according to Tschumi, anywhere; at La Villette if it meets another structure it simply attaches a fragment of itself and moves on to the next point; otherwise it ignores the existing and historical topography. His use of it is, then, a reminder of both the emptiness of the folly itself (most of those at La Villette have no function) and of the whole notion of genius loci, since if the structures have any reference at all, they are elsewhere, to Russian constructivism; the grid's immediate scope is shown to be placeless and limitless. Tschumi's design celebrates the end of a tradition, even while cynically relying upon it.[25]

35. Parc de la Villette, Paris.
Photograph by Emily T. Cooperman.

Yet the folly has other modern emanations, where site and its noumena are still explored and revealed. Finlay's work for public sites contrives for visitors some intimations either of local meanings or of larger meanings that can be still given a local habitation and a name. But the final example of two contemporary sites—in Germany and France—suggest how landscape architects have been drawn to invoke versions of the folly as a means of alerting visitors to the special, even noumenous, significance of place and have done so in ways that suggest a renewed wisdom in the understanding of genius loci.[26] In all these cases, the site could well have been left alone, anonymous, unmarked, and unremarked; it is also certain that none of the landscape architects would have sought to position his or her work within a tradition of garden follies. Yet that is exactly where we need to see it.

The disused steelworks in the German Ruhr are contemporary ruins, so there is no need to invent them. The whole site could, at vast expense no doubt, have been cleared away (many an abandoned industrial zone has been made to vanish, to be replaced with anonymous, bland greenery). But Peter and Anneliese Latz transformed the derelict and toxic site along the river Emscher into the Landschaftspark Duisburg-Nord. They allowed volunteer vegetation to absorb parts of the site, established new gardens in the disused bunkers, and celebrated the ruinous infrastructures by opening up walkways from which to view them and by encouraging new uses (climbing on the huge concrete walls, scuba diving in the former tanks). The park honors its past with these new potentialities, accepts the follies and crimes of industrialism with humor and skillful adaptation of its detritus, and above all rediscovers the landscape folly.

You can drive a truck from Turin to Barcelona and back without stopping anywhere except for gas or toilets: fuel pumps and restrooms look much the same everywhere these days. And the autoroute is of course engineered to be a safe but anonymous road sweeping past places that it can ignore completely: the signs that flash past the windscreen merely indicate the localities that your haste allows you to bypass and ignore. But even Italian and Spanish truck drivers, let alone motorists, do have to stop, and the French landscape architect Bernard Lassus answered a call from a private autoroute company to mark memorably one stop on that long anonymous trajectory. The result is that with the erection of two belvederes (see Figure 11) that take the form of the ancient Tour Magne in the nearby city of Nîmes, in each of which is placed a miniature version of the same Roman building, along with the reerection of a nineteenth-century façade of the Nîmes opera house, unwanted by Norman Foster when he redesigned it, those motorists and drivers who stop at this rest area have some sense of the place which their vehicles will bypass on the autoroute but which they can glimpse now in the distance.

ADAM AND EVE knew only one place, for a while, and had no need or desire to differentiate it from any other; it was both itself and everywhere else; its genius loci at once obvious and unremarkable. But thereafter both they themselves and their descendants have roamed the world, where differentiation of place became a necessary and sustaining instinct. From that original error, the *felix culpa* or (to coin a Latin phrase for fortuitous folly) *stultitia fortuita*, emerged a human concern to invest in whatever place chance or choice deposited them. More often than not they took their folly with them, made gardens, and inserted there some defining structures; it helped them to made sense of where they were.

Chapter 7

Jardins

Reflections on the Human Condition

This title ("Jardins: réflexions sur la condition humaine" in French) was given to me by the organizers of "Les Rencontres André Le Nôtre" in 2013, I suspect on the advice of Jean-Pierre Le Dantec, a writer on gardens. It was an event to mark the tercentenary of the great designer's birth. The three-day symposium at Versailles involved many excursions to sites not always designed by Le Nôtre, evening events in the Potager du Roi and in the Château, and, largely, discussions among participants of the role of landscape architecture in a modern political and community world. My own contribution seems to have been the only historical perspective.

THE VERY FIRST garden—whether you consider it as a mythological or as an historical site—was Paradise, the biblical Garden of Eden. But precisely at the moment when humans were banished from that place, they realized two things: first that it was indeed a garden, while before it had been the only place they knew, just an unexceptional place, full of animals and plants that they presumably thought were routine! Second, they discovered the *idea* of a garden: simply by being thrust from Eden into a hostile and alien world, they needed to work the land for survival and had to strive. This is clearly adumbrated by the mid-ninth century in the *Hortulus* (or *Liber de cultura hortorum*) of Walahfrid Strabus, to whom Jean-Pierre Le Dantec draws attention at the very start of an engaging narrative of French gardening.[1] But beyond places to grow what they could eat, humans eventually sought to accomplish a garden that tried to recreate the dream of the lost Eden. Over doubtless many years, the idea of a garden emerged from a comparison with other territories—agricultural land, mountains, and forests, wildernesses that nobody wanted to inhabit or enter into voluntarily, with memories of a long-lost paradise. We can see the realization of this idea in places where gardens, of one sort or another, have been established in very different territories—monasteries in the desert below Mt. Sinai, or medieval castles where dragons lurked outside and where, in a painting by Bernardo Martorelli,[2] even the small castle gardens outside the walls offered no protection unless protected by St. George.

The garden, then, was to be distinguished from other places. We know a garden when we see one, because we have known other places that were *not* gardens. We know a garden in part because we have experience of them and probably many of them, either by seeing familiar, daily ones—a front garden in the district where I live—or by visiting garden festivals at Chaumont sur Loire or the Métis Festival in Canada, or seeing radical or community gardens; even elite places like Versailles. It all depends upon the particular time and place of some human experience of gardens; but we nevertheless acknowledge what a garden is.

I suggest that we know instinctively when we are in a garden. The wooded pathway that we see in Figure 36 may be inside a much larger park, but it is instinct with the idea of garden—in its delicate fencing, its stepping stones over a marshy stream, and the sound of waters that we do not see in an image; but above all, by the fact that we have stepped into it, have crossed a threshold that is fundamental to the idea of such special places. The image is in fact of an area in the large park or garden that William Beckford created for himself at Sintra outside Lisbon in Portugal, and that was subsequently expanded and created by Sir Richard Cook. It is actually many things—a park that contains individual gardens and waterfalls (like this one), but also fountains, collections of different plants (ferns, scented flowers, roses), an arboretum, and an exotic mansion.

This adjudication of what is a garden and how it relates to its surroundings started of course much earlier. A miniature from René d'Anjou's *Mortification de vaine plaisance* of about 1470[3] shows us a miller waiting for the delivery of a sack of corn to his water mill; he owns a small *potager* or vegetable

36. The rill in the parkland of Sintra, near Lisbon.
Photograph by Emily T. Cooperman.

garden, walled and with a gate alongside the mill; an orchard, also enclosed with wattle work, lies across the lane: all of which personal possessions are set within a larger agricultural landscape with a farm, some perhaps uncultivated land, and in the distance a castle or maybe a town. The miller would know exactly which place was what (vegetable garden, orchard, field, town), but that knowledge was probably unconscious, or at least determined by virtue of some social instinct that told him his proper place within the hierarchical society of his time. Such of course was the advice offered by Piero de' Crescenzi, who distinguished between "large and moderate gardens of persons of moderate means" ("de viridariis mediocrium personarum magnis et mediocribus") and "garden of kings and other illustrious and wealthy lords" ("de viridariis regum et aliorum illustrium et divitum dominorum").[4]

It was perhaps only when the garden was conceived of and promulgated during the Renaissance as a self-conscious art form that new ideas of the garden were promoted and clearly distinguished them from other places, not solely by virtue of the social class they served, but also because they represented a different aesthetic dimension from other landscapes; though this was equally and often also a social perspective.

But even in the sixteenth century it was initially something of a puzzle to know how contemporaries would call what we nowadays call a garden and to find a word for it. Two Italian humanists clearly saw a distinction between agricultural land, or what we would call cultural landscapes of towns, ports, bridges, fields, and so on, and the wild world of gods or savages. Both saw gardens as something different from either fields, wastelands, or wilderness: Bartolomeo Taegio and Jacopo Bonfadio—as far as I can see writing independently of each other—wrote, "L'Industria d'un accorto giardiniero, che incorporando l'arte con la natura fa che d'amendue ne riesce una terza natura" and then added "a cui non saperei dar nome" (gardens were the result of the industry of local people connecting nature with art in such a way as to make something that I'd call a third nature, but I do not know otherwise how to name it).[5]

This third nature (the "terza natura") was opposed to and yet derived its inspiration from the second or cultural landscape and from the primary world of the gods (wild and mysterious). Materials were the same—rivers, trees, topography—but changed and augmented and formalized: thus the river that enters the gardens of Vaux-le-Vicomte from adjacent agricultural land was canalized as it ran through the site, but then exited in its own form, winding through the water meadows. At different times and in different cultures, landscape architects have refined, epitomized, transferred, or left untouched the materials they use within gardens.

The triad of natures continued to be represented in both verbal discussions of gardens and, most clearly, in engraved images of the sites: sometimes this representation of the three natures was little more than diagrammatic, as in

Art

Natura

CURIOSITEZ
DE LA NATURE ET DE L'ART

37. The frontispiece to *Curiosités de la nature et de l'art*, by
Abbé de Vallemont, Paris, 1705. Private collection.

the frontispiece to the book by Abbé de Vallemont (Figure 37), where we see a garden sandwiched between fields and mountains; and the agents who gesture to this landscape, Art or Science and Nature, also are placed within a rough, unformalized topography. More sophisticated images of specific estates, like engravings by Kip and Knyff around 1700, still saw the whole landscape as an intricate mix of a third nature near the house, more agricultural land, including orchards, beyond, though still organized for human consumption, and then wilder hills in the far distance. This landscaped layout of estates paralleled the diagrammatic lines of de Vallemont's image, and it was a pattern widely used throughout Europe in the seventeenth and eighteenth centuries. That this precise delineation of spaces disappeared as a visual format in the following centuries is clear, though not universally so—J. M. W. Turner's view of Niton on the Isle of Wight from 1826 pays attention to exactly the same sense of a gradation of sceneries from garden terrace to distant hills.[6] Yet if the eye or the artist did not actually see and record this triadic structure of landscape, still part and parcel of a human's sense of the territories he or she observed or moved through, that was because we have expanded the idea of the garden to almost absurd proportions. Anything could be deemed a garden.

Today there are many types of gardens, as a witty compilation by Hans Ulrich Obrist makes clear.[7] And in each of these gardens—and he gives us *four* pages of them!—we should notice, first, that each kind of garden has its own typological character—a Dirt Garden is *not* a Corporate Garden, for example—and, second, that, notwithstanding this typological plenitude, we still assent to, we acknowledge, a garden when we see it under its various forms and uses. Third, in even the oddest of garden types (an airport garden, or a cruise garden—and, believe me, there is a forest park on the cruise liner *Oasis of the Seas*, just as there is forest garden inside the Bibliothèque Mitterrand in Paris)—there is something special about each of them, not least because it is distinct both from other gardens and from whatever surrounds it contextually. And what has clung to each of these hundreds of types of gardens is that the garden is a place apart, even if we depend upon our familiarity with other sites and places.

This special quality depends, obviously, on a whole cultural range of responses. What is special for me is not the same as it would be for, say, a farmer; for an Englishman, not the same as for a Frenchman: thank heavens, it would otherwise be a very boring world! That perception must, though, alert one to the dangers of a global landscape architecture today, when too many famous and prominent architects fly around the world and make gardens that could, often, be invented for just about anywhere with little attention to the invitations that issue from some precise locality. But one element they all have in common is the effect—literal or mental—of some luminal moment, when you step into a garden from a place that is not a garden.

The specialness of gardens was an early quality that has never been entirely lost, though it blurs often into nostalgia and sentimentality. Gardens in ancient Greece were created as special, indeed sacred, places; they no longer exist, but were depicted on coins as groves dedicated to some deity or to the genius of a place; they were sites to which people were admitted by rank, even by gender, and often the trees themselves were carefully chosen; activities within them were also carefully prescribed or proscribed.[8] Other cultures, too, relished the garden as a sacred and special place, as with Shinto shrines in Japan.

Many centuries later, when the first white men discovered the Yosemite Valley in California in the late 1850s, they found it a sublime and marvelous place, for which they struggled to find an appropriate description that acknowledged the sacred: it was a cathedral, a garden, a park, a book of scripture, a natural sculpture gallery—though one irremediable pragmatist said it was just "a large horse trough." American preservationists celebrated its "pristine beauty and wilderness," though even Emerson saw its utilitarian possibilities as a "graceful park for use and delight."[9] Painters, like Albert Bierstadt in 1864, found Yosemite a strange, haunting, and numinous place. It is what the French would call, justly, "un haut lieu." What few if any of the white explorers seemed to recognize was that Native Americans, the Ahwahneechee tribe, had seen the valley as instinct with mystery and had named the surrounding mountain peaks with sacred names, which the white men promptly renamed with the most banal of labels, like Inspiration Point or Half Dome.

While I am not, it must be confessed, a religious person, I always sense, if not a sacredness, at least a specialness of many places that I'd call a garden. And I have felt it in Yosemite, as I have in the European Alps. But an instinct for the sacredness of garden spaces lingers still: when the American landscape architect Lawrence Halprin sketched his first idea of the memorial garden for FDR in Washington, D.C., he labeled a portion of it as "sacred," as opposed to the profane areas of its immediate surroundings.

But gardens offer many services, and the performance of the "sacred" is only one of them. Another is their strongly pedagogical role—though as a professor and academic I am somewhat loath to deny a sacred role to pedagogy! Gardens have always been where we learnt consciously or by instinct. Adam and Eve learnt the hard way how to honor a garden only when they'd lost it. Renaissance humanists and later landscape architects saw the world outside gardens as material and lessons for the making of third natures: the range of the Apennine hills was invoked to name the huge statue of a giant in the Medici park of Pratolino that was called the Appennino (Figure 38). And when humans learnt to wander outside gardens, they found that this larger nature was also a teacher, though they had almost certainly learnt to read it first within the enclosed forms of a garden: thus Joseph Wright of Derby painted several

38. The statue of the Apennines at Pratolino.
Photograph by the author.

Englishmen in the countryside outside gardens, like Brooke Boothby (in the Tate Gallery), actually holding a copy of Rousseau's *Les rêveries du promeneur solitaire,* as he reclines and meditates in the woodland of his estate.

But it was perhaps the early European botanical garden that was the most conspicuous place of learning and education, as it gathered into one protected and symbolical world the treasures of a larger one—from America, Africa, and Asia. This was where professors taught students in the gardens of the University of Leiden's botanical garden, and where John Parkinson in England gathered together the researches for his botanical compendium: it was a *Theatrum Botanicum,* where the riches of the natural world are displayed in each of his corners of his frontispiece, and also "performed"; for he imaged it on the stage of London's Globe Theatre, supported by the Pillars of Hercules, with Adam and Solomon as the actors, representing the first gardener and the first scientist.

This pedagogical impulse of gardens is profound and widespread. It blossomed into a variety of other forms, still allied with the idea of the garden, for, as many contemporary landscape architects affirm, the garden is the *terminus ab quo* from which the making of all other landscapes derive; even when the architects are more preoccupied with parks and non-gardenesque sites, they celebrate the garden as the source of their work: Peter Latz has argued that "amateur movements [in garden making] play an important role in garden culture" (something he shows clearly in the park of Duisburg-Nord); the American Garrett Eckbo wrote that "garden design is the grassroots of landscape design. . . . Private garden work is really the only way to find out about relations between people and environment"; while Bernard Lassus, at a conference in Sicily in 1981, asked why "the garden, the hypothesis on what, from yesterday and today, will be perpetuated in the sensory approach of tomorrow and its new ways to touch and be moved—is not such a garden before all else philosophical?"[10]

And we may follow the garden idea into a whole host of sites that were never thought of until the late Enlightenment: public gardens like the Englische Garten in Munich—as opposed to aristocratic ones opened only occasionally; national parks like Yosemite, and the whole spectrum of Parcs Naturels Régionaux de France; international exhibition grounds like the Philadelphia Centennial Exhibition in 1876 or the World Columbian Exposition in Chicago in 1893 (where part of the grounds were designed by Olmsted);

botanical gardens and arboreta that have blossomed into a variety of new sites from Shanghai to Bordeaux, in all of which the garden idea is clearly seized and exploited. We have gardens on rooftops—one of Le Corbusier's *Les cinq points d'une architecture nouvelle* of 1926, though of course there were, much earlier, the hanging gardens of Babylon; we have hanging gardens—parterres hoisted vertically onto the sides of buildings; or we have gardens that descend into the earth (as at Parc de la Villette), and gardens that are not even natural, like Isamu Noguchi's marble courtyard for the Beinecke Library at Yale University, or the insertion of wonderful steel cutouts, where the metal plays dialogues with the adjacent planting.

One of the excitements these days of garden making is not only that gardens are resumed into a variety of different kinds or typologies of site but also they sit cheek by jowl with a variety of other typologies.[11] Sometimes these are subsumed within one site—for example, the park of Duisburg-Nord by Peter Latz + Partner rescued a disused and moribund steelworks as a parkland and inserted into it gardens, athletic events (making use of climbing walls and tanks for scuba diving), and an amphitheater, and yet it retains the sublime frissons of the derelict factory. A modern parkland extends the idea of a garden and includes other examples of gardens, within a larger, cultural program.

This reformation into parkland at Duisburg-Nord is perhaps one of the most dominant landscape activities of the past quarter century. Derelict and often toxic industrial sites, decayed waterfronts, and disused harbors have been seized for public gardens and parks. The garden or landscape conceived as infrastructure is conspicuous through the world, and thus extends the idea of the garden into new cultures and new, even unexpected, places. We know and delight in the display of images of gardens where there are no gardens, at least immediately adjacent: tiles on the façades of nineteenth-century houses in Lisbon, painted landscapes on the exteriors of a housing development in Uckange, or the whole panoply of garden imagery that is used in advertisements to seduce us.

When I published a book on garden culture a few years ago I had to debate with my publisher, who wanted to call my book *The World of Gardens*; but my book was not about what happened in gardens, not the world within gardens, but the fact that there was a world of gardens in different times and places throughout the world—hence the need for my title, *A World of Gardens*. Yet when all was said and done, gardens in China, in Japan, in Mughal India, and in Europe do tend to speak—in their various tongues—about the garden *tout pur*. The range of cultural inquiry does not, then, entirely inhibit us from reflecting on gardens generally. So we might finally remind ourselves of the lines by Jacques Prévert found in the Jardin Jacques-Prévert at Saint-Germain-des-Vaux in Basse-Normandie, which argues that we must look with a good eye to recognize a garden: "Si vous ne le voyez pas d'un bon œil, le paysage [dit jardin] n'est pas laid. C'est votre œil qui peut être est mauvais" ("If you don't look with a good eye, the landscape—or garden—isn't ugly. It is your eye that is perhaps bad").

Chapter 8

Between Garden and Landscape

In memory of MICHEL BARIDON

This essay responds to a remark of my old friend, Michel Baridon, on a distinction between gardens and landscapes, which he thought William Gilpin had been the first to discover. In further exploring this notion, I find more dialogue than distinction between these landscape events.

On dit qu'un Jardin peut être un Pays, main on ne crée pas un pays.
(One says that a garden could perhaps be a countryside, but one doesn't create a countryside)

Si un lien existe entre paysage et jardin, c'est celui, paradoxal.
(If there is a link between garden and countryside, it is indeed paradoxical)

IT IS A great pleasure to celebrate the work of Michel Baridon, whose distinction in the field of garden and landscape history is beyond doubt. With Michel, it was always an exciting and challenging experience to exchange ideas on this topic. And in that spirit, I want to engage two themes that were central to his work and thinking: the relations between garden and landscape, and, then, his role as a specialist in eighteenth-century studies (*dix-huitièmiste*). But—given his abiding interest in contemporary garden design—I want also to extend that eighteenth-century discussion into a more general commentary on that relationship between garden and landscape in modern landscape architecture.

The last writing by Michel Baridon, published posthumously, was an introduction to a French translation of William Gilpin's *Observations on the River Wye,* edited by Frédéric Ogée and issued by the Presses Universitaires de Pau in 2009.[1] In his introduction, Baridon writes: "And it is an essential fact that he [Gilpin] does not describe a landscape as if it was a garden. That is a veritable discovery" (p. 14). It is true that Gilpin did "discover" the pleasures of the wider landscape for innumerable contemporaries and provided careful advice on how to experience them, especially if tourists wished to view or even depict them in sketches. Where I am less convinced is that Gilpin's own experience in gardens did not direct and shape his observations in the larger field, even if perhaps he does (or seems to) describe a landscape as if it were a landscape garden. So I thought it worthwhile to explore in some depth what exactly was the relationship in the later eighteenth century between gardens and landscapes, which Michel Baridon seemed to consider different experiences.

WE MAY approach this topic from two directions: from Gilpin's own, early account of his visit in 1747 to the gardens of Stowe, and then from the first of his later observations, those taken on the river Wye during a journey more than twenty years later in 1770 and published twelve years later still.

In the first account, the *Dialogue* on Stowe gardens, we see clear signs of Gilpin's not only responding to the designed landscape garden itself but equally reading it in ways that bias him toward what one of his characters calls "rough Nature." These are the nondesigned or cultural landscape of fields and agriculture—"our well-cultivated plains . . . are certainly not comparable to their rough Nature in point of prospect" (p. 24). In the later *Observations on the River Wye,* I suggest, we find Gilpin responding to the configurations of a nondesigned scenery as if he were still, at least occasionally, in an extensive landscape garden like Stowe.

The character Polypthon in the Stowe *Dialogue* says that he has experience in "visiting what was curious in the several Counties around him" (p. 1); while that may include landscape gardens, it clearly also takes in larger territories, for he dilates upon his travels in the northern counties of England and Scotland; similarly and conversely, Gilpin's narrative of his Wye excursion begins with his stopping to view the landscape garden at Caversham House, where (despite cavils) he notes the work of "Capability" Brown, whose "great merit lay in pursuing the path which nature had marked out" (Section I), and also his inclusion of visits to the landscape of Persfield on the way down the Wye (Section V) and remarks on designed sites at Foxley, the home of Richard Payne Knight, where he writes of the "form of the grounds about it, and the beautiful woods that surround it," and on the much praised landscape estate of Hafod in North Wales (Section VI).

Upon entering the grounds at Stowe, Polyphon, ignoring the immediate foreground of buildings, responds to the extensive and varied "view," and throughout the tour of the gardens he cavils at much of the architectural and sculptural insertions (complaining of Dido's cave, "'tis built of hewn Stone!" [p. 14]). Generally, he prefers what he terms "offskip," or distant backgrounds, to close-up and foreground details. While some of his grumpiness is doubtless contrived by Gilpin to activate the dialogue with his more conventional companion, the enthusiasm for northern scenery seems genuine rather than provocative. What is more, he seems concerned to negotiate how that taste meshes with the experience of Stowe. His "rough Nature" is couched in a conventional, picturesque vein, and his implied wanderings through any landscape are presented by jumping from item to item of "beautiful [or characteristic] Objects," (p. 24), a concept he uses in his *Observations*. But it is a concept that he often misses in specific places like the scenery around Ross on Wye: "It is marked by no characteristic objects" (Section I). Yet, just as his characters move around Stowe in pursuit of these beautiful objects and collate them in their imaginations, so the traveler on the river Wye applauds and composes his own selection of beautiful objects: an "amphitheatre of mountains" (Sections III and VIII) animated by local herds and "smoking cottages" and with "views into the Country"; then a steep precipice, gloomy, with a foaming river at its foot; and a particular "place" on the river Eden, which is "as fine a Piece of Nature, as perhaps can any where be met with," incorporating a small anthology of picturesque forms—"garnished Rocks, shattered Precipices . . . Woods, . . . elegant Vales," and "enchanting Views" (p. 25).

Not surprisingly, Polyphon at Stowe argues radically for bringing the larger countryside into a landscaped garden, as when he opines that were he a nobleman "I should endeavour to turn my Estate into a Garden, and make my Tenants my Gardiners: Instead of useless Temples, I would built Farm-houses; and instead of cutting out unmeaning Vistas, I would beautify and mend

Highways" (p. 45). And he quotes lines from Milton's "L'Allegro" in praise of an extensive and undesigned countryside (p. 53). A similar, yet reversed, claim is made by his companion, Callophilus, who expounds the more conventional view: what he needs is "the Garden [to be] extended beyond its Limits, and take in every thing entertaining that is to be met with in County, Villages, Works of Husbandry, Groups of Cattle, Herds of Deer, and a variety of other beautiful Objects [that] are brought into the Garden Plan" (p. 52). Such a concern is satirized later by Thomas Rowlandson (when Dr. Syntax encounters a mob of animals in his search for the picturesque); yet Callophilus's notion does not impact the general instinct to draw the larger landscape into gardens.

This taste for such larger prospects, learnt and enjoyed from within designed parkland and gardens, was certainly widespread by mid-century. We might think of William Kent's garden at Rousham redesigned in 1739. In a letter describing the pleasures of that site for its absent owners, the steward, Macclary or Clary, singles out the extensive rural countryside that is seen from within the garden: thus we look out at "five pretty Country Villages" and a "pretty Corn Mill," to meadows with "all sorts of cattle feeding, which looks the same as if they were feeding in the Garden."[2] Such a taste for long views and for calling the countryside into the garden—in Alexander Pope's terms—would soon ensure that this wider and further nature was explored for its own sake. But in the meanwhile the taste as well as the understanding of it seem to have gained ground in such places as Stowe and Rousham.

Switching to Gilpin's *Observations on the River Wye*, we feel some distinct continuities with his earlier experiences at Stowe. Granted that Welsh landscape is much more extensive, that its scenery frequently lacks focus, or, as he says, "the scene wants accompaniments to give it grandeur" (Section III) and that the time taken in its exploration is much longer, and granted, too, that his central concern is to instruct a would-be artist in picturesque techniques and in the choice of subjects, for which unmediated territory is the true source, and which he tries to present in his own engraved views; nevertheless, he often seems to invoke his own earlier behavior at Stowe. The parallel is endemic, of course, generally within the eighteenth-century culture of landscape: both the landscape gardener and the landscape painter must learn how to "perfect" nature, so it is not surprising if much advice for one activity also suits the other. On the Wye trip, Gilpin complains both of nature's lack of foregrounds and backgrounds that would frustrate a painter, but these were also an issue for the earlier visitors to Stowe; for a landscape garden designer was equally obliged to see that both near and far worked within the "whole."

Throughout his observations on the Wye Gilpin presents Nature as an artist herself, if sometimes insufficient ("Nature . . . seems only to have chalked out her designs" [Section XII]). If she is there an artist only drafting in chalk, at other times she is credited with the active production of more complete and finished landscapes, like any gardener as well as painter: Gilpin insists that Nature disposes and shapes; that she is the producer of forms, and that she introduces rockwork, or may opt to reduce it. In these emphases of Gilpin's we may recall Alexander Pope's famous passage in the *Epistle to Lord Burlington* on the genius of the place, where the responsibility for shaping the landscape is ambiguously distributed between the place itself and its designer. Like Nature herself, Time too is proactive, says Gilpin: "Time with its lenient hand may hereafter hang new beauties upon these hills, when it has corrected their heaviness, by improving . . . their foliage" (Section X). Furthermore, Gilpin will use landscaping terms—"a noble terrace" or "lawn" (Sections IX and VIII)—about unimproved or unmediated terrain. He will write that a view "unfolds itself" (Section III), just as incidents presented themselves in the gardens at Stowe ("What kind of a Building have we yonder that struck our Sight as we crossed that Alley?" [p. 26]). This merger of experience and response, of discovering items and then of declaring a response to them, is most acute when Gilpin writes about the famous picturesque parkland of Hafod in North Wales: its landscape obviously lent itself to his particular enthusiasm for an extended design that celebrated the picturesque site while ensuring that its beauties were accessible along different circuit paths—"through this variety of grand scenery the several walks are conducted." Yet overall, he has conducted his own "walk" down the Wye Valley as if he were at Hafod. And his route down the Wye would serve as a model for many tourists treading in his footsteps, with his *Observations* in their hands, just as his own *Dialogue* on Stowe would guide subsequent visitors there.[3]

But it is also in his larger, more conceptual concerns that Gilpin reveals his affinities with landscape architectural theory and practice. Responding to a particular territory, he is nevertheless especially concerned to pronounce on the categories that might guide response; one such moment is his dictum: "The ornaments of the Wye may be ranged under four heads: *ground, wood, rocks*, and *buildings*" (Section II). This echoes Thomas Whately's categories in *Observations on Modern Gardening*, published the very same year that Gilpin wrote about the Wye: Whately writes: "Nature, always simple, employs but four materials in the composition of her scenes, *ground, wood, water,* and *rocks*," then adding: "The cultivation of nature [i.e., landscape design] has introduced a fifth species the *buildings*." Both writers then enlarge upon each of those categories, in Gilpin's case the "water" theme being subsumed in his actual mode of travel by boat down the "mazy course" of the river itself. Both writers address the need for "character" in a given scene, a technical and key term in these discussions.[4] Gilpin does so in lamenting that the Wye near Ross provides no "characteristic objects," that is, structures that would determine the particular "idea" of a place; Whately by devoting half a dozen pages to distinguishing different characters and how they may be achieved in landscape design.[5] Gilpin himself points out that buildings are a better and more useful, because deliberate, adjunct for creating character in artificial gardens than in natural landscapes, which he himself addresses at Dynevor Castle, Neath Abbey, or Tintern Abbey.

One sometimes wonders whether Gilpin even had a copy of Whately with him on his excursion (or at least consulted one while preparing the piece for later publication), or whether, alternatively, Whately had knowledge of Gilpin when writing at more length and from the point of view of a landscaper about Persfield and Chepstow.

THE DIALOGUE between garden and landscape that Baridon underlined guides my investigation of Gilpin's writing. But that dialogue was but one moment in the *longue durée* of landscape taste and criticism. Not that earlier, as well as later, commentators did not distinguish between the specific terms of garden and landscape, they did; but the exchange, the dialogue between them, the sharing of experiences across the ha-ha, through a grill, or even, in earlier times, beyond the walls of palace or castle, was of paramount importance. During the eighteenth century, we need to realize, the gardens of Stowe were but a small part of a much larger estate and plantation (Figure 39). And in modem times, despite a strong rearguard action to repress or denigrate the garden among ecologists and landscape architects, the cross-fertilization of landscape architecture by garden thinking and practice is still among our liveliest concerns and topics.

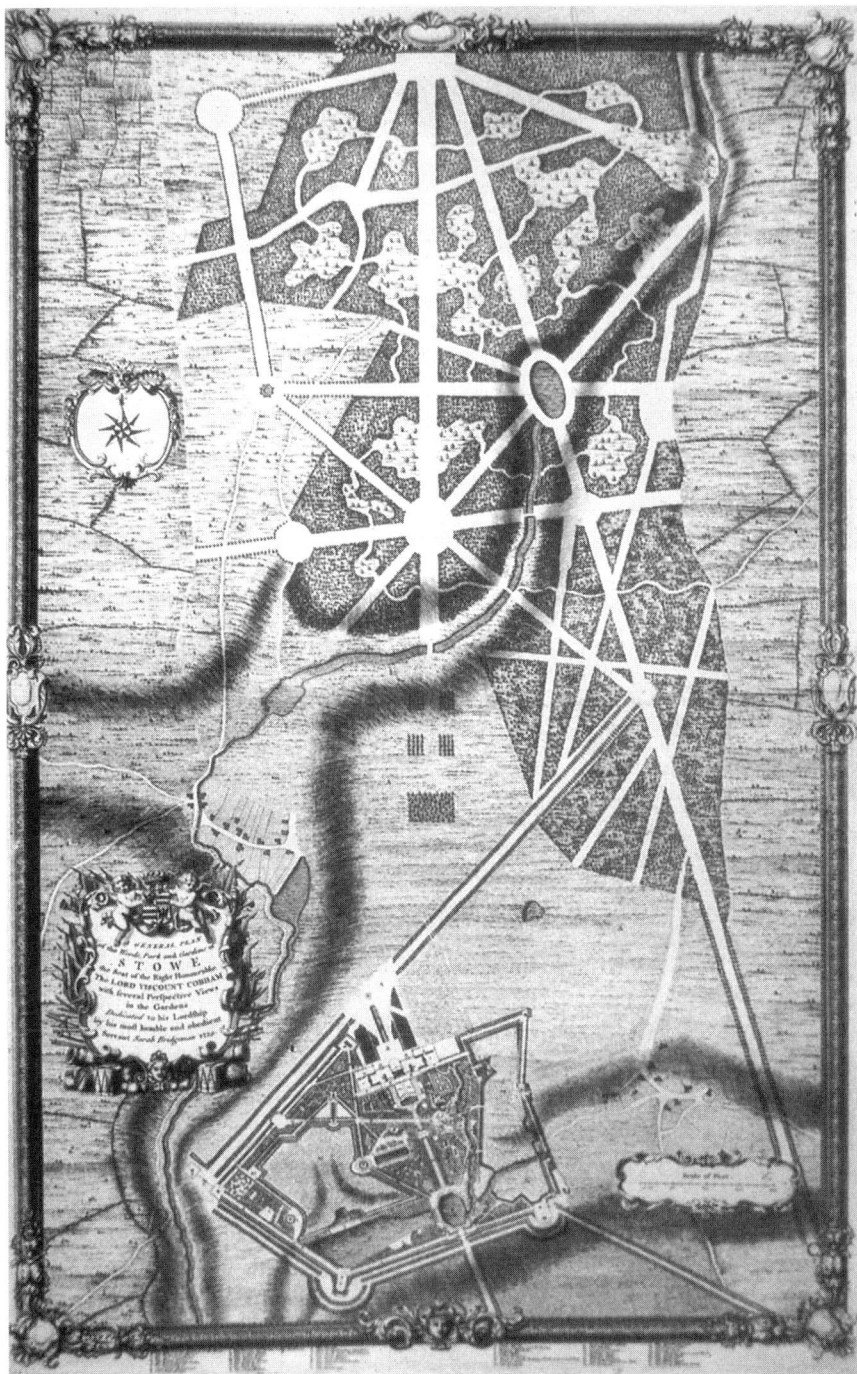

39. Stowe, a plan of the whole estate, with the garden itself at bottom left, next to the cartouche, 1739. Private collection.

So I wish to expand further upon this issue, looking backward and forward, concluding with some reflections upon the role that gardens continue to play in our modern thinking about landscape architecture. In 1962 the International Federation of Landscape Architects (IFLA) was addressed by Bruno Zevi, who called in question the dependence of landscape architecture on the garden: "Too many books and essays on landscape architecture are concerned mainly with gardens. Is this right, or does it demonstrate, that the philosophy of landscape architecture has to be brought up to date? The transition from city-design to town planning took place a long time ago: the same cannot be said of the transition from the architecture of gardens to the architecture of landscapes. Do you feel, that the time has come to establish a distinction . . . between garden design and landscape design?"[6] I suggest that Zevi's parallel between town planning and landscape architecture is misleading and flawed.

The garden has always involved the identification of a given space, the enhancement of that space, at times busy and fussy, but also occasionally sparse, with both built structures and the deployment of natural species, and a connection between its own special and significant space and forms with the surrounding territory that often lacked that mode of concentration or formalisms. This garden space is more often than not enclosed, as was most obvious in medieval examples, and it was set off and approached by conspicuous and even auspicious entrances, liminal moments of threshold or archway. Sometimes the outer areas were still visible over walls or from battlements, or they were sensed even if invisible—sensed, that is to say, from within the garden by virtue of having arrived at this inner sanctum from the larger world outside. It is this intimation of a special place that marks the idea of the garden, and it is this same identification and formation of space that should mark landscape architecture, which needs to be identified and experienced as just such a special place. If it is not so marked, or at the very least unmarked by the sense of having arrived at a place somehow resonant or significant, even if the approach is blurred or obscure, then the landscape has failed. In short, no landscape architect designs a landscape that nobody remarks upon, that does not present itself as in some way remarkable.

It is this exchange between an inside and a different outside that characterizes the idea of a garden. The exchange may be physical—an entry, a liminal threshold into a new world; or it may be visual—when you glimpse from inside the special space the larger and perhaps more ordinary world beyond its confines. Outside may be different—even very different—from inside, so that the world beyond is deliberately opposed to the interior forms, security, and safety of the inside. But the exterior/interior dialogue may be more subtle, more eloquent of graduated space between inside and outside; it may even share materials, forms, and functions, which, translated into the garden space, recall by their reformulated or improved aspect their originals outside. The dialogue or distinction of different characters was mooted very early in the Italian Renaissance.

I have written elsewhere about how, during the late sixteenth century a couple of Italian humanists choose to describe the art of gardening, then coming into strong prominence throughout Italy, as a "third nature."[7] This neologism derived from their sense that the world of garden making was significantly different from the world of what Cicero in his *De natura deorum* (*Of the Nature of the Gods*) called a "second nature" (*alteram naturam*) to distinguish the world that men and women made from the sublime world of unmediated nature and sacred places of the gods. This second nature—towns, agriculture, infrastructures like ports, roads, and bridges—was a cultural activity, whereby humans organized their daily lives and made the world useful for themselves. The third nature, therefore, was an extension of the two other worlds into a newer and even more finished world of place making. Yet this "third" move did not imply a disjunction from the second or even the first nature: rather, it gave garden makers the opportunity to take elements of the larger world and rework them in garden form. It could incorporate references or even imitations of the first nature (mountains and "wildernesses"); or it took from the ordinary human and material world such things as rivers, and straightened them; or it took woodlands and made them into elegant groves, agricultural hillsides were terraced in more regular forms, caves and *antres* were made into often elaborate grottoes, and water in all its effects was made to cascade, jet, and even play music.

This understanding of the provenance of garden elements was made clear both in seventeenth-century engraved views and in the commentaries that garden writers proposed. Most engraved views of mansions and estates were taken from a bird's-eye perspective, in which the different zones of control were clear and palpable. Close to the house was the most intricate and detailed garden, then came groves, orchards, and less structured or less busy plantations, and beyond was the world, maybe cultivated, but otherwise wild or barren. The informed eye recognized these gradations and the exchange between different types of treatment of the land.

But the eye could also be trained to notice them: the third Earl of Shaftesbury wrote out exactly such an instruction for his house at Wimborne St. Giles, of which we get a hint in the elaboration of his portrait in a published volume.[8] He saw that gardens near the mansion steadily gave way to less and less ordered shrubberies and trees, and the eye was eventually "guided" through these intermediate zones of the garden, with trees and hedges removed so as not to hinder the view outward. He asked for sightlines to be established whereby large topiary bushes—"larger Pyramids" and "Tall Globe-Yews"—be succeeded by the "intended middle rank" of Scotch firs and "Cypresses [to] make a Contrast."[9] Finally, with "no Prospect for them to hinder," the sight is taken further into the immediate countryside beyond the garden: "The last row of Winter Greens to be continued by other plain Holly Trees of any sort . . . at large distances only for ye guiding of ye Eye up that Hill and so to ye end of ye reset Fields where ye great old Yew Trees stands." Thus, within the garden, the eye was tutored to register the forms and characters of trees and bushes so that, once arrived outside it might recognize the true forms of natural materials. In time, such "tutorials" so educated the eye that by the end of the eighteenth century it came to *prefer* what lay outside the achieved and manicured garden; and in that education Gilpin played an important role.

Between garden and landscape, then, we can establish many connections and dialogues. For William Gilpin, his visits to gardens like Stowe were the chance to attend carefully to a designed world, the understanding of which he would then carry into the larger world. He never gave up visiting gardens, as the Wye *Observations* make clear, but when his own career led him into observations and books on landscapes throughout England, Scotland, and Wales, he was right to value landscapes over gardens—indeed, it was necessary to do so. For him, it was indeed a "veritable discovery" to be able to describe a landscape in ways other than as a garden. But for us, I would suggest, both modes of thinking about territory were as much a vehicle of exchange or liaison as some opposition between them.

Chapter 9

Ekphrasis

Déjà Vu All Over Again

> *It has been argued that all criticism of visual art is essentially*
> *ekphrasis. But what can be repeated in words about a garden*
> *or landscape is not the same as the garden or landscape, though*
> *it may direct us to what we should see and learn from that*
> *experience.*

THE AMERICAN BASEBALL player Yogi Berra, famous for his malaprop-
isms and absurd formulations, once remarked that something was "déjà vu, all
over again." I use this in my title as a means of alerting readers that my subject
focuses upon how an ekphrasis, in my case ekphrases of gardens, functions
by way of repetition yet equally by way of difference; like the writer in Jorge
Luis Borges's story "Pierre Menard, Author of the Quixote," who rewrites Cer-
vantes's novel exactly, using the same materials, but whose new text, however
precisely repeated, is never exactly the same.

It may well be that what I am to offer on ekphrasis is just that—déjà
vu—once more, over again. I run the risk of adding absolutely nothing to
the huge body of work on the topic of ekphraseis that has been generated
over the past twenty years, to which material I hope I am properly indebted.[1]
I am also in danger of repeating over again what I said in the talk that I
gave in Nice some twenty years ago on the topic "Ekphrasis of the Garden."
However, I resume this theme again in memory of Michel Baridon, who had
invited me to that conference in Nice and subsequently published my piece

in his journal *Interfaces: Image Texte Langage.*[2] But I take up that theme in a different way.

I wish to try to sketch one fundamental aspect of my topic: that different objects—paintings, sculpture, architecture, or gardens—elicit (or should elicit) very different ekphrastic responses; we must learn to discriminate between different kinds of descriptive practices. So, first, what does a garden require? Or what is needed in a proper and useful response to it, and, second, how might such descriptive practices shape or determine the reception or afterlife of a garden? For while theory may be useful, it is surely important to insist that theory is there to illuminate works of art (in this case gardens), rather than to show how any given art work will illuminate theory.

Ekphrasis déjà vu is, in some sense, just that, twice over: you see, for example, a picture, and then you "see" it again in a poem. And when you return to the picture itself, which I am assuming one does, you see it over again in the light of the poem. However, the issue is exactly what that "over again," that "déjà," really means, both as regards the poem itself vis-à-vis the picture, and then as regards the picture viewed afresh as a result of the ekphrastic intervention. What we call the afterlife or reception of the painting in the poem should now in some measure incorporate and augment our understanding of the painting, just as an art historical critique of the painting redetermines how it may be viewed. This "afterlife" in the poem and its reception of the *painting* is as much an effect of the ekphrastic move as the *poem* itself. Yet this is not much studied, this *re*-vision of the object (the painting) in the light of the poem: we tend to read the poem in the context of knowing or looking at the painting; but rarely do we let it affect how we look back at and think about the painting. The ekphrastic moment, or poem, is generally—if you like—an end in itself; it uses the painting as its starting block, as a mode of inspiration, even influencing the poem's action, but it does not, so to speak, repay its debts to the painting. But we can, I think, take that further.

In his essay "Art History as Ekphrasis,"[3] Jàs Elsner argued that art history is not possible without ekphrasis, that art history is "ultimately grounded in a method founded on and inextricable from the description of objects," and that the "*enormity* of the descriptive act cannot be exaggerated or overstated" (my italics). This article is itself enormously refreshing, even something of a relief to those who work in word and image studies, where the activity of description is undeniable and inextricably linked to our performance of it in *words*. So I want to take up Elsner's argument and direct it now to garden history (which he himself does not mention). This will be, in part, simply a reaffirmation of his ideas and their application to the study of gardens, but also a chance to scrutinize ekphrastic descriptions as they relate specifically to gardens and garden history.

Now in discussions of gardens and garden history we encounter a variety of special features (that is, aspects of this art form that do not apply elsewhere). To start with, the garden is never "static," as Michel Beaujour claims (except in very rare circumstances, when we might be able to see a small garden at a glance, in window boxes, for example, or in a Wardian case).[4] The garden is not something we can generally "see," as when standing before a picture, an architectural façade, or a sculpture. A sculpture certainly is not static, and should usually be viewed in the round, but it still enables a response that holds the illusion of it as a static object. But the garden's essence is precisely composed of its double existence in time—its own life in history and our own need to explore a garden in time, since its spaces require that we move through them, and this in its turn entails an extended response. When I first visited the gardens of Stowe in Buckingham, with William Gilpin's *Dialogue* in my hand, it required more than seven hours to complete the itinerary. Moreover, the growth of a garden's natural forms subject it to a variety of changes, mostly its gradual plenitude over the years (one thinks of the lines from Alexander Pope's *Epistle to Burlington*, "Nature shall join you, Time shall make it grow / A work to wonder at—perhaps a Stow"); but there are also the threats of decay and dissolution. Even a small garden that we could take in at one glance is liable to change over time, through the seasons, even hour by hour, as a result of light and atmosphere. Further, some elements in a garden are also *not* translatable into an ekphrasis: smells, sounds (to a huge extent), the physical impression of what one sees or whatever surface one is walking on (gravel, moss, grass), the simultaneity of sensations (the awareness of the air and the breeze), and our natural ability to observe a landscape in a wide-angle gaze (we don't all look through the viewfinder of a camera).

Some garden elements do seem, however, compatible with other art forms. We expect to find "meaning" in gardens, which we do variously, sometimes by observing their formal means, sometimes by confronting various inscriptions directly, sometimes by extrapolating from "silent" or "dumb" items in them. Yet in both instances—even in reading an inscription—we are not observing the garden's "objecthood" *tout pur* but are drawing from it, or imposing on it, our own tendentious ideas, some of which are determined by our own cultural assumptions, some by our understanding (or misunderstanding) of historical circumstance, which may also be culturally driven in our own case. In that sense, Elsner is right to imply that all art history as ekphrasis is tendentious. We may like to think that much contemporary garden description has a certain foothold in objective reality, because it so often incorporates elegant and often wonderful photography that adorns most books on the subject these days: but here, again, I'd accept Elsner's argument that these photographs are just an ekphrasis within an ekphrasis—some photographs will illustrate the same point as the text but are still themselves an interpretation of the garden in their choice of subject, angle of vision, and so on. Those that seem to have no consonance with the text provide nevertheless their own take on the garden. (In fact, the tendentious hold of the garden photographer seems to be bolder and stronger than photography of other art objects, probably because garden photographers rarely work in tandem with the authors—for instance, I am astonished by how much "posh" garden photography completely omits any people and fails to address how a garden may be received by critic or visitor).

In garden analysis we also invoke terms that are borrowed from relevant disciplines—formal or informal, picturesque, baroque, modernist, naturalism; but these too are found not in the object, the garden, but in our verbal and often long-standing invocation of critical language, and many of these terms are really awkward when used in garden analysis. Finally, as Elsner notes, one very fascinating aspect of ekphrastic description is that it makes the particularity of the object more general; garden ekphraseis do this in large part by assuming or drawing into their precise description our larger, or more conceptual, ideas of gardens.

When I published the original essay from the Nice conference in *Interfaces* I prefaced it with two quotations, of which Paul Valéry's "Seeing is forgetting the name of the thing one sees" continues to resonate with me. I presume he does not mean, if he were to focus specifically upon gardens, that the name per se of a garden—Versailles or Chantilly—is forgotten, but that the richness of the site and the multitude of its demands upon us may overwhelm the name by which we refer to it. We know Versailles as a place, but just how do we really know the Versailles when we see it in person and on foot, or later in the mind's eye, or in representations of it? Or, since Versailles is so enormously complex, as Michel Baridon has handsomely reminded us in his *Histoire des jardins de Versailles* and other writings, let us take an apparently much more simple and certainly smaller garden, like Rousham, in Oxfordshire, by William Kent, from 1739.

Many people of course don't even know the "name" of Rousham, but the name can indeed easily be forgotten by our visitation of the garden, by our absorption in its small but telling insertions, its pathways and rediscoveries of vistas and view sheds. So the name of even a small site like Rousham may certainly be eclipsed; but a description or ekphrasis of Rousham also may leave its mark upon how we see it, so that the name we arrived with or attach to that site is no longer the name we take away with us.

I will pause awhile now to consider this particular garden, on which I have frequently practised my own ekphrastic descriptions,[5] where for a while I lived in a cottage on the estate, and on which there have been a limited number of good descriptions from which I can draw my examples. But my thinking began a few months ago as I was trying to formulate my thinking for this text, and I stumbled upon a new book of poems dedicated to that garden at Rousham. It was entitled *Her Leafy Eye* (Reading: Two Rivers Press, 2009). It devotes twenty poems to Rousham, mostly by writing about specific features there, though it occasionally responds to a series of more general gardenist items like "folly," "espalier," "topiary," and "the Genius Loci." Its author is Lesley Saunders, "an award-winning poet." Her foreword explains that the "eighteenth century 'picturesque' landscape gardens at Rousham" have "inspired" the poems: that description of Rousham as "picturesque" seems designed to encourage us to see the garden as a series of pictures, which might therefore be especially apt for ekphraseis. But the volume also contains some images by Geoff Carr, which presumably work to reify Rousham's "picturesqueness" in another medium alongside the poems. Carr's note says that his computer-generated images "refer" directly to the poem that brought the image into his mind's eye, "often arriving completely resolved and in no need of further thought" (*sic*!). Carr is a garden and design practitioner, a filmmaker on gardens for the BBC, and a creator of garden sculpture and garden furniture. Finally, along with an oddly miscellaneous and incomplete bibliography on Rousham, the foreword of two pages expounds the "Furor Hortenis" (the garden craze) of the eighteenth century. It notes, among its picturesque elements, the loss of topiary in the eighteenth century. This round-up of typical "picturesque" gardening is fine, if somewhat sweeping, but little of its account is taken up in the poems that follow, and Saunders even includes a poem now on "Topiary" (p. 37), though this had been expunged from the *furor hortenis* and does not feature at Rousham. Overall, then, the site of Rousham is over-whelmed with commentary, both discursive and imagistic, descriptive and imaginative; what Elsner calls its tendentious descriptions are clear for all who read the volume.

The whole point of this volume seems to be that it is based on the Roush-am gardens. Even if you don't know the site, there is a rough map, annotated with the numbers of the poems dedicated to it, and concluding with a final poem, *en face*, that is entitled "Visit." But that final poem is unspecific, apart from the final line about leaving "a note in the box / as they go" (a reference presumably to paying a fee for entry,[6] or does it mean a note of thanks or com-mentary in the visitor's book?). It could be, in fact, any garden "visit"—indeed, the mown lawn sprouting with stones in the first stanza doesn't jibe with Rousham's bowling green, and easing the "timber over the jamb" in the second doesn't fit anything I know about that particular visit; the sensations of dust, damp, names on a wall, and "amethyst fire" are simply baffling.

Two of the briefer poems may help us forward. The first takes its title from the Scheemaker sculpture *Lion Attacking a Horse* that graces the end of the bowling green. The poem indulges in fanciful associations—a unicorn, grappling lovers in the moonlight, and the honeybees that will inhabit the lion carcass hereafter (only if the horse wins, I presume). Frankly, it seems a less than energetic encounter with the sculpture, evading any sense of why it might be there—we'll return to reasons for its placement later. Another poem also concerns a particular move of Kent's in designing the gardens in 1739, when he moved the Lion and the Horse to its present position, so that its loca-tion presides over the view and leads us to it. For Kent also deliberately took our eyes into the countryside by a whole series of incidents—a mill gothicized with flying buttresses, and an "Eyecatcher," as it is called, or a triumphal arch, also gothicized, on the far hillside (see Figure 32). That poem is printed op-posite one of Carr's computerized images, but the image and the naming of the actual Rousham feature itself are really the only clues as to what the poem might be saying, and (absent those particular clues) there is nothing that ties the poem to this location: the first line of the final stanza—"I have been try-ing all my life / to see beyond the horizon"—might be true of far horizons in general, but in this case the Kentian arch is designed to pull our eyes out to the far hillside rather than to "see beyond" it.

So in this case Elsner is more than right—that the ekphrastic effort at particularity tends rather to embrace generality. While the titles of most of these poems do refer to items at Rousham, they neglect anything local or particular. Essentially nothing about the poem "Rill" intersects with the actual rill at Rousham. There is nothing about the Walled Garden or the grotto that speaks of, or returns our interest to, those specific moments at Rousham. It is certainly true that such poems might bring to bear our larger notions of garden-ness upon the Rousham visit, but they do not even do that.[7] Therefore I am puzzled about this volume, which offers to address Rousham but does not engage with it and certainly, in my view, does not return us to the garden with any new insights.

Now, we could argue that poems are not the best medium in which to confront a garden; but are there better descriptions of Rousham, or, rather, do other ekphraseis succeed in doing better with how we might respond to Rousham? We are fortunate in having a small group of very influential and worthwhile descriptions of Rousham, and these can help us; one, in particular, from the year 1760, for all its oddities, provides a wonderful ekphrastic opportunity, and I shall come eventually to that.[8]

In modern commentaries Rousham "suffers" from an overzealous focus by art historians and literary historians (including myself) on the "meaning" of the gardens, so that the garden seems lost within the thickets of learned discourse. Mostly, this requires privileging an iconographical narrative of items in the gardens based primarily on the specific identification of the sculptures, as if the meaning of the garden were contained only within these isolated features; many other sculptures that are acknowledged to be elsewhere in the gardens are otherwise ignored in the commentaries; so, even more, are the spaces *between* all the sculptures (for what can one say about them?). When we are asked to draw meanings from specific objects like sculptures, we are often encouraged to go outside the garden, to consult emblem books, or (in one case) a "rather obscure legend" regarding Proserpina in the Greek topographer Pausanius, or accept a strained attempt to explain the topography of the garden according to cultural geography with Gothick elements to the north, an "Egyptian pyramid" to the east, and a classical zone or ancient Roman site to the south.[9] Somehow the commentaries seem often at odds with the experience of the site itself, despite the photography or woodcuts that authors supply to illustrate the place; other narratives involve internal contradictions, or miss any sense that a garden is liable and open to multiple associations, especially when the claim is based upon one obligatory route around the gardens, for there can be, in fact, no privileged circuit "intended by Kent."[10] In the tight, oddly shaped garden, tricks of perspective and unexpected sightlines play a crucial part in teasing the visitor, and it always seemed to me to be a whim that took me one way or another when I visited the garden.

Some items are certainly convincing and control our attention: the arcade known as "Praeneste" takes its single sequence from the multileveled range of arches at the Roman Temple of Fortune at Praeneste, the modern Palestrina. The Lion and Horse at Rousham echoes a similar sculpture at the Villa d'Este, where it overlooks the Roman campagna just as Rousham's group presides over the Oxfordshire countryside (we know that Kent moved the group to that position from beside the house, where the landscape would not have been visible). The Dying Gladiator, originally designed to be placed on a Roman sarcophagus, clearly references Rousham's dying patron, General Dormer, and may well contribute, along with the horse attacked by the lion, to the mortuary tonality of the whole place, which other commentators make their main theme. But contrariwise, Venus, as a garden deity, presides over her valley, watched by a faun and Pan lurking in the shrubbery, which has given several commentators a plausible reason for relishing an understandably eighteenth-century lascivious moment:[11] I once argued that this might have been a reminiscence of book 6 of Spenser's poem *The Fairie Queene*, a poem that Kent would later illustrate; but the point is that you don't need to know that reference or allusion for responding to Rousham.[12]

But many things don't "fit." Gardens can certainly be melancholy places, and we may, if we like, take the river Cherwell at the bottom of the garden slope as the river Styx that bordered the classical Elysian Fields. But there are also happier prospects: not just the dying Gaul or the savaged horse, but the luscious and lascivious Venus, and views out toward a "triumphal" arch and the Temple of the Mill, which feature in what Horace Walpole called Kent's "prospect, *animated* prospect" (my italics).[13] Items that are said to be "inappropriate" to the theme of the Elysian Fields are nonetheless skewed so that they fit the holistic narrative of the relevant iconography. Many other sculptures that do not fit the narrative are either ignored or explained by saying they give the garden an antique air (which is a more likely gloss).[14] Confronted with the statue variously described as Apollo, or as Antinous, or simply as a "colossal" figure, commentators choose to reject Antinous, the beloved of Hadrian, because (i) it is nowadays presumed to have been "rather meaningless" as a Renaissance attribution and (ii) Apollo would anyway better fit the Rousham profile.[15]

There is and was a river Styx, so called, in the Elysian Fields at the garden of Stowe, where Kent designed the buildings but arguably was not involved in the overall landscape. But it does not make it reasonable that the same identification works at Rousham: there is no inscription at Rousham to point the way, and David Coffin has to work hard to confine his narrative to this idea. His identification of the Cold Bath, where Proserpina spent half the year, confined to Pluto's realm, allows him to identify its position halfway down the sloping ground: "Hence there is the *suggestion* [my italics] that the actual river Cherwell below the garden symbolizes the river Styx which bounded the classical underworld of the Elysian Fields. Here at Rousham, then in contrast to Stowe, Kent *did not have* [his italics] to manufacture a new river Styx."[16] But the problem is that the identification of the Cold Bath with Hades as Proserpina's Cave is indeed "manufactured," a fantasy of the steward, called Macclary or Clary, writing in the 1760 letter, where he says he designated it as Proserpina's Cave himself and embellished it with figures, but "my Master not likening [one of the figures], I chopt them all down."[17] This whim of the steward's hardly suffices as a basis for creating yet another River Styx in Oxfordshire.

Indeed, it is Kent's garden design, not Macclary's, that is relevant, and Kent—however steering or directed by his patron—worked in certain ways that we can determine. He was deploying Dormer's own collection of sculptures, not selecting his own selection of relevant images; he was also working in a garden that had been laid out earlier by Charles Bridgeman; yet he was also clearly seduced by his own memories of nine years in Italy, with its recollections of Palestrina, the Villa d'Este, and the grottoes of the Villa Aldobrandini, to which he probably gestured in the Vale of Venus. Furthermore, there is no certainty that any one narrative or iconography would take precedence over another; indeed, items may have offered themselves variously to different visitors. General Dormer may well have seen the lion attacking the horse as a mortuary reference, but it seems more likely that Kent himself would have recalled its presence at the Villa d'Este (where it symbolized the lion of

Rome's subjugation of the horse, Tivoli). Yet Kent's implied allusion to how Italian scenery was referenced in Oxfordshire must have been deliberate, since Kent moved the sculpture from beside the house to its position on the rim of the garden slope, and the Roman campagna, as he would have known, isn't anything like Oxfordshire. Equally, the multistoried terraces at Palestrina (or Praeneste) are diminished by the *single* Kentian arcade at Rousham—quite properly, anything bigger would be disproportionate to the scale both of the site and of England itself. A Roman triumphal arch, also apt for a famous soldier, must needs be given a distinctly Gothick style for an English general.

Furthermore, we need to take into account Kent's own impish and even satirical perspective, most likely suggested to him by Alexander Pope, with whom he was on very good terms. Pope's writings made much of the *alterations* that had to be made to classical poetry to fit them in English verse (notably in his *Imitations of Horace*), and he mocked the pretensions of the English dunces by pitting his own mock-heroism against the austere giants of Homer's and Virgil's epics. Kent participated in a similar play at both Stowe and Rousham. For instance, besides Kent's recall of Italian items in a reduced and diminished English way, there is something satirical in what he did. Below the statue of Venus at Rousham is an inscription lamenting the good life of an otter hound (Figure 40)—David Coffin links that immediately to the mortuary theme; but Kent was always drawing dogs in his garden sketches, frisking or even pissing against a wall at Chiswick. At Stowe Kent celebrated another dog on the rear of the Temple of British Worthies (Figure 41): Coffin says the Stowe foxhound is there to "be memorialized . . . along with the virtuous Englishmen," and for Rousham he argues that the hound's "burial" at Rousham makes clear an association with the Elysian Fields theme. Kent's playful and irrelevant use of dogs suggests a much more mocking undercurrent than one that "supports" the other iconography. Coffin seeks to link every item in the garden to the theme of the Elysian Fields: he even "presumptuously" (his word) points out that Homer's *Odyssey* (book 4) placed the Elysian Fields in the west, beyond the "known, inhabited, living world," which is certainly where Rousham's "new garden" was in relation to its house.[18] The slight problem is that there was nowhere else on the estate for the garden to be put except to the west!

Finally and briefly, in the strange and somewhat naïve letter of 1760 written by the steward, hoping the owners will return from inhabiting another

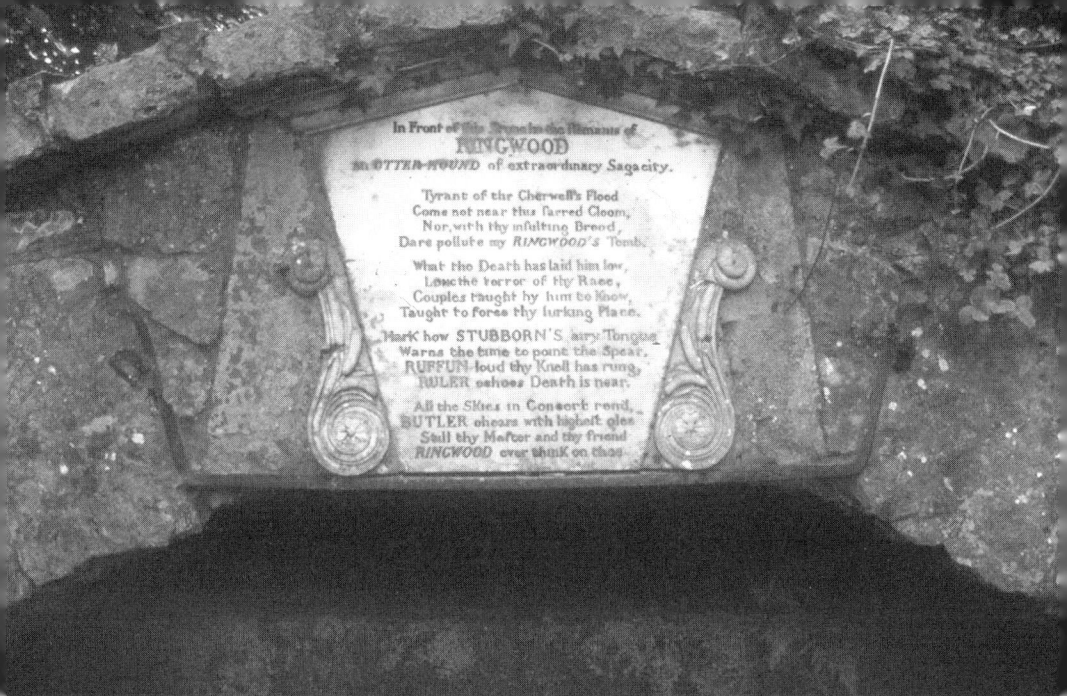

40. The memorial to the otter hound below the statue of Venus in Rousham's Vale of Venus. Photograph by the author.

estate, Rousham does emerge with a much more convincing and richly nuanced ekphrasis. Sure, maybe even interestingly, the steward misses the Apollo, just as he also does not name the Praeneste terrace, though we know from the house accounts that this was how it was called; but neither Apollo nor Praeneste has an inscription, so he was presumably left on his own. However, the steward does also faithfully note almost every sculpture by name or description, though without any commentary on them, and he lists far more items than are conventionally cited by commentators. Yet what Macclary (or Clary, as he later called himself) does spend considerable time on is what usually gets neglected in modern discussions, because it seems to play little role in the design of the garden. Instead he emphasizes three key elements: views in and without the garden—what you see around you as you walk or sit; a whole range of agricultural and country matters, which he lists with far greater enthusiasm than the statues; and finally his endless celebration of its planting. These emphases do most emphatically speak to the effect or the reception of the garden as he and the absent owners would find it, and it continues to have an impact on how we respond to the gardens.

41. The Temple of British Worthies in the Elysian Fields at Stowe. The inscription that one finds by exploring behind the temple is a mock celebration of another worthy, but as one reads the lengthy inscription we discover that the worthy is Fido, another dog. Photograph by the author.

Macclary's insistence on the planting was, we know from other sources and contemporary contacts, William Kent's signature effect; it seems routine for us now in visiting gardens, but Macclary's insistence should make clear how innovative and astonishing was Kent's rich and careful under-planting of all sorts of trees. Macclary notices "Oaks, Elms, Beach, Alder, plains and Horsechestnuts" as well as evergreens throughout, where walks were "backt with all sorts of Flowers and Flowering Shrubs," with "a great veriaty of evergreens and flowering shrubs," and remarks that "here you think the Laurel produces a Rose, the Holly a Syringa, the Yew a Lilac, and the sweet Honeysuckle is peeping out from every leaf" (there are other references along these lines). Plantings change over the years, obviously, but we still need to respond to a similar "infrastructure" of plants. Macclary is also passionate about the essential, rural ambience: we look out beyond the garden to "five pretty Country Villages" and a "pretty Corn Mill," to meadows with "all sorts of cattle feeding, which looks the same as if they were feeding in the Garden"; within the estate itself he notices a paddock stocked with "two fine Cows, two Black Sows, a

Bore, and a Jack Ass," "as pretty a sett of pig Stighs as aney is in England," kitchen and flower gardens where the fruit is lovingly detailed, fishponds, a dairy yard, and the church.[19] Mutatis mutandis these elements are still all there today, and the adjacent farmyard is still very much in use.

In Chapter 2, "Near and Far, and the Spaces in Between," I suggested how we might response to the fullness of a garden experience like Rousham. And while ekphrasis tends to focus on specific items in a garden, Macclary's prose responds to what we see and know, certainly, but also to a host of impressions that Macclary figures to be an essential part of that experience or one that he wishes Rousham's owners to appreciate. If ekphrasis of gardens is about what we see, it must also take us back into the garden itself and revisit it in the light of whatever the verbal descriptions of it have provided. So it is that, since the Nice conference in 1993, I have somewhat distanced myself from Michel Baridon's editorial commentary where he divided "les pesanteurs disciplinaires" (disciplinary thinkers) between "les Littéraires" and "les historiens de l'art." For gardens are not simply, if at all, the "site of [the] conflict" that W. J. T. Mitchell, also at Nice, saw as the warring field of word and image operations.[20] The garden is surely not, as Mitchell pronounced in his book *Image, Text, Ideology*, "a protracted struggle for dominance between pictorial and linguistic signs, each claiming propriety rights on a 'nature' to which only it has access."[21] I'd say rather that the nature of garden art escapes, even as it complicates, the many *interfaces* of its particular elements, and it thus allows us an enlarged entry into what Michel Baridon also termed "tous les domaines de la connaissance."

Chapter 10

Preservation in the Sphere of the Mind

Duration and Memory

> *Memory and the role of association are prime contributors to
> how we respond to gardens and landscapes. But we have lost the
> classical, rhetorical traditions of storing and utilizing memory,
> so we must find ways of allowing both the designer and the
> visitor to share the layers of memories and associations that
> linger within the form of each design.*

IN A CHAPTER of *Civilization and Its Discontents* Sigmund Freud addresses
the issue of how much and how long the human mind can retain memories.
This "general problem" is, as he puts it, a question of "preservation in the
sphere of the mind."[1] I reread his chapter, in which he argues unsurprisingly
but almost triumphantly for the complete retention in the human mind of
everything that has been formed there, when I was preparing to talk on architecture and memory at Georgia Tech.[2]

No subject has been as discussed among writers on landscape architecture with such enthusiasm as its ties to memory. Two substantial collections
of essays—neither, unfortunately, in English—have explored the connections
with apparent thoroughness: a colloquium during the early 1990s in France
produced *Le jardin, art et lieu de mémoire*, while a collection of Italian essays
entitled *Il giardino e la memoria del mondo* was issued by the Florence publishers Olschki in its series "Giardini e paesaggio." I mention these partly to
note that there *are* relevant critical works available—and landscape studies

are absurdly blind to work in other countries and other languages (as those two volumes themselves nonetheless reveal in their solidly Euro-centric references)—and partly because their contributions do not in the end seem to address adequately the topic engaged with here. Most of the inquiries so far conducted into the associations between landscape and memory are grounded in historical invocations of classical rhetoric: the famous study by Frances Yates *The Art of Memory* (1966) is the distinguished exponent of how the art of memory—the *ars memoriae*—was understood and practiced in medieval and Renaissance times.

But—to put the matter now succinctly and bluntly—the traditions and habits by which classical rhetoricians and their successors explained and practiced the arts of memory seem to be useless in our very different culture: a culture with no educational insistence on training memory and apparently far less need to do so systematically in an age when we have abundant paper and pencils (which the ancients did not possess), as well as palm pilots, portable recorders, video, photography, tapes, and so on. And more important than that: we inhabit a culture that seems to have so little in common with the ancient rhetorical devices of, for instance, emblems and allegorical figures, which might have signaled shared ideas and concepts but which can no longer be employed today except in art historical scholarship; in short, such a compendium of references or arsenal of shared general knowledge cannot be counted upon as a lingua franca in communication. Bernard Tschumi himself declared that the project for the Parc de la Villette "aims to unsettle both memory and context." And he quoted Nietzsche in one presentation to affirm that "the world for us has become infinite, meaning that we cannot refuse it the possibility to lend itself to an infinity of interpretations."[3]

I want to inquire, briefly, into this breakdown of classical traditions of memory systems, as a prelude to asking what modes and mechanisms of memory are available these days both to landscape practitioners and to those who experience their work. I'll focus upon one very illuminating incident that occurred at a watershed of modernity in the eighteenth century.

IN 1747 Joseph Spence, who was a professor of both poetry and modern history at the University of Oxford, decided that a sufficient knowledge of Roman divinities, their names, attributes, and powers, was lacking among both students and the general public; so he wrote and published *Polymetis,* which went through innumerable editions until 1774 (suggesting indeed that there was need and demand for his work). In it he assembled all the verbal descriptions and visual imagery he could find on each deity and gathered them—statues, inscriptions, medals, and so on—in a series of appropriate temples scattered around a large landscaped garden. As visitors proceeded from temple to temple they'd learn, or refresh their memories, about the characteristics, behavior, attributes, actions, and associations of each deity, including the various aspects of any one, like Apollo. It was a memory bank of classical lore and legend, or (if you like) a huge peripatetic encyclopedia, or (alternatively) some reserve collection of texts and slides in a modern university library for a course on classical mythology.

The very year in which Spence published this guide to the nomenclature and attributes of Roman gods and goddesses a young clergyman called William Gilpin, later to become famous as the theorist and popularizer of the picturesque, visited the gardens at Stowe, which must have seemed in its profusion of temples, statues, and inscriptions not a bit dissimilar to the imaginary landscape of the *Polymetis*. Gilpin subsequently published an account of this visit in 1748 in the form of a dialogue that contrasts two kinds of reception of the Stowe site and its dense array of iconography.[4] One visitor seems to possess an instant recall of all necessary knowledge by which to negotiate the gardens; the other prompts his friend by constantly asking about the stories represented in paintings and the meanings of the series of temples; on some few other occasions the less informed man himself registers and identifies subjects—"taken from the Fairy-Queen I dare say; they look like Spencer's Ideas" (p. 6). On several occasions "inscriptions . . . explain the Designs" (p. 13) and allow disquisitions on the topic or subject identified (William Penn, for instance, p. 38). But gradually there develops a distinct contrast between Polyphron, who hankers after meanings and identifications, and Callophilus, who responds more to formal effects, vistas, and prospects (it is he who identifies a structure of "whimsical appearance" as the "Chinese House" [p. 26]).

Yet the contrasts are not so stark as that suggests: Callophilus finds "a kind of Emblem" (p. 31) simply in the shady walks of the woodland groves rather than in some symbol or sculptured item. His ability to instruct his companion also suggests that he has mastered meanings and references as the mechanisms of garden meaning, even as he moves beyond them (he knows that his companion can purchase a guide to all the inscriptions and garden imagery at the local inn—implying that he has done his own "homework"). Throughout, whoever displays competence or is baffled by what is encountered in the long excursion through the gardens, whether identifications are precise or whether something only "puts one in mind of some generous patriot in his retirement" (p. 40)—that is, provokes a very general idea, it is clear that a landscape like Stowe was designed for and expected to provoke and sustain a constant flow of conversation that drew upon an assumed body of shared memories.

Gilpin highlights precisely the range of comprehension possible to a mid-eighteenth-century visitor in a landscape garden richly endowed with items that the previous forty years had deemed perfectly readable. This range stretches from the communication of precise and knowledgeable information to a much more informal and even vague apprehension of what the visitor encounters, impressions more than distinct memories. As the *Dialogue* closes, however, the one who has been so concerned to know exactly what reference, what story, what incident he is faced with, is allowed to celebrate the garden as "a very good epitome of the World" (p. 58), understood as a variety of incidents that will satisfy the very different characters that the various garden scenes propose. It is as if, by the end, even this character, Polypthon, can accept a measure of expressive and affective design.

ALL THIS resonates with a distinction familiar enough today. Marc Treib can usefully stand as its representative spokesman when (in writing about the Woodland Cemetery in Stockholm) he opts to cast aside "erudite references to history that demand an educated visitor" in favor of "significance [that] does not depend on interpreting iconography."[5] Yet what this significance does depend upon is not very clear, but seems—for Treib—to be instinctive responses only to the *forms* of design. I am not so convinced that we need retreat so far. While we are certainly heirs today of the distinction proposed by Thomas Whately in 1770 between "emblematic" gardens, with readable imagery and a vocabulary and syntax apparently shared by all visitors, and those that promoted "expression," or the far more personal responses of the sensitive and solitary imagination, this does not mean that we have totally lost our memories and can no longer exercise our imaginations. It is a familiar claim that both education and the diversity of the world in which we live—despite its globalism—deny us any commonality of reference, even that this very globalism reduces to a bare common denominator the few signs and references we have in common. Nonetheless, while we probably live in what I would call (playing off Yates's *Art of Memory*) an art*less*ly mnemonic world, it is not a world without memories. And these memories will include a range of possibilities unimaginable in the eighteenth century, even though faced with a loss of shared imagery, and clearly unimaginable by Treib, for whom there seems to be nothing in the memory bank that can use "iconography" or "erudition" to the extent that he relies on the conscious act of "interpretation" of forms. Here we might recall, even if we cannot now linger upon its suggestive scope, Sigmund Freud's discussion of the mind's resources, in particular its particular ability to preserve memories like some palimpsestial model of the ancient city of Rome: "In mental life nothing which has once been formed can perish—that everything is somehow preserved and that in suitable circumstances . . . it can once more be brought to light" (pp. 16–17).

WHAT IS clear is that for both designers and those who benefit from and experience their designs, there exist skills, even arts, to activate and indulge our capacity for imaginative memories.

First, I'd like to put aside on this occasion the topic that should receive adequate treatment: memorials.[6] By their very nature, many or most memorials are established within communities that recognize what is at stake, what is being recalled, and understand the location and syntax of the invention. While it is true that the Vietnam Veterans Memorial, for instance, has generated an often extreme range of responses, nobody is ignorant of what is memorialized there, even if both the mode of commemoration and its "take" on the war in Southeast Asia have been debated. It is also worth reminding ourselves, however, that some memorials at least can lose their resonance over time—the emblematic case, I suppose, is the worn gravestone and its corollary, what we might term the "Elegy Written in a Country Churchyard" syndrome of "mute inglorious" denizens of innumerable graveyards about whom we can recall nothing whatsoever.

The far more problematical issue is what meanings or memories can be communicated by contemporary landscape architecture when design does not specifically invoke some event or famous person (like the FDR Memorial in Washington, D.C.). Yet landscape architecture without memorial function is not, surely, devoid of what we might call resonance; I mean that excellent design work (there is no point in focusing on the less than good) is characterized among its other aspects precisely by such an "aura" or resonance that activates memory, memory that in its turn depends upon both imagination and knowledge in its recipients. Nietzsche popularized the idea that we cannot learn anything that we do not already know, so one strategy by which our memories are activated on a landscaped site is by the design reminding us of something which was up to that point lost, forgotten, or repressed but which, now released, is worked upon by the imagination, and since this is a question of memory, by the historical imagination (in the broadest sense).

We need to look at matters from both the designer's point of view and the visitor's, which do not always—nor perhaps do they need to—coincide. The designer has basically two strategies: to predetermine meanings and try to communicate them, counting upon his or her skill at producing forms that will release in visitors a range of memories and meanings that approximate his or her own; alternatively, the design might eschew all effort to insert or encode meanings, trusting presumably to a series of willingly interactive respondents.

From the visitor's perspective, we may imagine some visitors who consciously but sympathetically apply their own resources of memory to an encounter in such a way that they appreciate some, many, or even all of the meanings intended by the design (if such *were* intended). But equally or alternatively, the visitor may simply exercise his or her free association, drawing upon associations and memories that the designer might never have considered, and thus come to "fill" the site with his or her own more or less rich and rewarding ideas.

We have sufficient experience of all these modes and responses: the student at a final review or the designer making his or her pitch to a client or jury may elaborate on the "meanings" that the design supposedly incorporates, but in those circumstances the visitor's share (I rework E. H. Gombrich's famous phrase in *Art and Illusion*, "the beholder's share") is largely ignored or postponed. But once a site comes into existence, there is the possibility of its visitors being guided in an interpretation of some precoded meanings. We all have used or seen visitors using guidebooks that spell out what may escape or be missing in their own our minds and memories, prompting them in ways that the site itself cannot readily do. But we have also experienced extraordinary flights of fancy in response to some site or design: it happens all the time in academic criticism! But it also happens in ways we can only guess at (unless we eavesdrop) when people visit and respond to sites with their own indi-

42. The Vietnam Veterans Memorial, Washington, D.C.
Photograph by the author.

vidual resources of experience, knowledge, and memory. Some sites that have
been in existence for a long time, especially through cultural changes, provide
fascinating examples of fresh readings, as verbal and visual records accrete a
palimpsest of receptions. Even the Vietnam Veterans Memorial (Figure 42)
can be seen as having already acquired a multiplicity of responses; contested
memories, yes, and some more preferable than others, according to what you
bring to the experience. Another example would be the centuries-old habit of

responding to ruins by completing their structures in word or image, filling the vacancies with perhaps new associations, restoring fragments after the visitor's own mental recollections and designs.

Seen from this, the visitor's or receiver's, perspective, the possibilities are vast. But there are resources for the designer to call upon that can rescue him or her from being trapped between the rock of community design and the prescription of meaning, on the one hand, and, on the other, the hard place of arguing for some universal human kitty or reservoir of reliable memories. An obvious case is the invocation of materials and forms that recall by intensifying locality: Halprin's cascades in Portland are an abstract recollection of mountain streams, and Kiley's wonderful Fountain Place in Dallas gathers swamp cypresses and a descent of waters in ways that remind us of (but do not try and replicate) Texan swamp landscapes. Another move is to concentrate—not crowd, but epitomize—forms that seize the imagination by the force of their own presentation: here, again, Fountain Place, establishing its own strong identity as a precious enclave within the urban hardness and heat, allows anyone to dream and think within its virtual enclosure.

SOME DESIGNERS, confident presumably with the durability of memory, have of course taken the initiative and directed reaction and reception while invoking the rich resources of their own art. Here are two examples. At the edge of Ian Hamilton Finlay's garden of Little Sparta near Edinburgh visitors come upon a fence fragment descending into the lochan, on which is inscribed the single word PICTURESQUE (Figure 43). To which there are many responses, all of which require some mnemonic agility and activity on their part: they can laugh at the apparent unpicturesqueness and see a joke at the expense of this tired old warhorse of a concept; or they can acknowledge its tribute to the fascination with decay (what the painter John Constable called "old rotten banks, slimy posts");[7] perhaps they might recall the vogue for basing landscape design upon painterly models—though then wondering whose paintings are imitated here, as scenes earlier in the garden had recalled Dürer and Claude; or, if we are alert to the context and to Finlay's fascination with revolution, we might find a more strenuous reference to the famous British exponents of the picturesque—Gilpin, Richard Payne Knight, Uvedale Price, and perhaps Humphry Repton—who are, not unimportantly, contemporaries with those other revolutionaries, Saint-Just, Rousseau, and Robespierre, whose lives and works are by no means negligible let alone picturesque in the cant usage of that term. The marvelous success of this small intervention, I suggest, is precisely that it opens up a whole anthology of memories.

One project from 1997 onward by the Swiss landscape architect Paolo Bürgi draws upon history even as it relies upon the extraordinary context of its mountain site. At Cardada above Lugano a geological observatory (Figure 44) gathers and presents the materials for a review of geological time, notably recalling the collision of the European and African continents: Bürgi calls it "un grande scenario, una storia fantastica," which his proposal seeks to bring

43. Ian Hamilton Finley, "Picturesque," at Little Sparta. Photograph by Emily T. Cooperman.

44. Paolo Bürgi, the Geological Observatory, Cardada, where the visitor gazes toward a mountainside, split millions of years ago by the shifting of the African and European tectonic plates, samples of which geology are lined up on the platform. Photograph by the author.

home to visitors by activating historical imagination on a suitably dramatic site. And lower down the mountain a breathtaking promontory is cantilevered into the void above the forest; along its pedestrian surface the "attention of the visitor" is directed to a series of embedded images—from DNA molecules out of primordial seas to the signs and markings of our own ecosystems.

What characterizes all these sites is their confidence in the mnemonic capacities and capabilities of visitors, and that these memories endure. They reach out and draw us into *their* world, proposing an agenda of meanings for which our memories are either likely to be already primed or in need of some refreshment. What we cannot know, unless we are prepared to undertake this research more systematically than has been done heretofore, is whether, on sites like these at Little Sparta and Cardada, people create their own version of the site from other ideas, associations, and memories.

"ARCH, n. an architectural term.
A material curve sustained by gravity
as rapture by grief"

*I use the occasion of responding to a small bridge, designed
by Ian Hamilton Finlay at Little Sparta, to explore how we
come to attach feelings to places and to meditate further on the
plausibility of Ruskin's "pathetic fallacy."*

THERE ARE A couple of shelves in my university's arts library with books on bridges, a few touching on their engineering, but most on displaying the rich range of their forms and even uses. I have always thought that Great Britain has a wonderful array, dating from very early medieval times, and one book by J. M. Richards, *The National Trust Book of Bridges* (London: Jonathan Cape, 1984), celebrated this plenitude. Its glossary defined "Arch" as: "A curved structure spanning an opening. It can take various shapes: semi-circular; segmental (part of a circle); elliptical (part—usually half—of an ellipse); pointed (two curves meeting at the crown)" (p. 200). I will contrast this definition with the quotation in my title, which is taken from Ian Hamilton Finlay and is inscribed on a small "arch" that crosses a little stream at Little Sparta, his garden in Scotland (Figure 45).

Finlay is fond of invoking definitions that one might find in a dictionary: so this is defined as a noun ("n") and as an "architectural term. A material curve sustained by gravity" (clear enough); but then a somewhat unusual deviation of the definition is glossed as "rapture is sustained by grief." The arch

45. Ian Hamilton Finlay, "Arch," at Little Sparta.
Photograph by Emily T. Cooperman.

at Little Sparta is also a bridge. Also, there is another "bridge" here, with an inscription that declares, in both directions, "THAT WHICH JOINS AND THAT WHICH DIVIDES IS ONE AND THE SAME." It too is placed over a small streamlet. Another bridge, just to keep you up to speed with Finlay's bridges, is an elegant glass one at Fleur de l'Air, a garden that he designed for a private client in Provence (see Figure 48). This one is inscribed with the words ARK/ARC. In his commentary on this in Finlay's book on that French garden, Harry Gilonis writes: "Crossing a bridge is not without its moral implications, as Heidegger has pointed out. . . . Bridge-crossings prefigure our own final journeys." He also notes that ARK (as in Noah's ark), like its homophone, arc, is archaic English for arch.[1]

Now my theme is not to discuss Finlay, or any architectural term as such (obliquely that may occur), but to discuss bridges.[2] Particularly bridges in gardens and landscapes. What, if anything, may we say about them, except that they keep our feet dry when crossing a stream? Or in the case of Provence, a bridge will help us over a rather inhospitable and deep gully, and provide a moment of security in a tough terrain where wild boars roam.

Let me begin with a simple, historical point, which is the premise for what follows: bridges only appeared in European gardens during the eighteenth century. It is curious that in all the books on bridges I looked at, the commentary on bridges *in gardens* was infinitely small or nonexistent, and never addressed the historical moment of their appearance: yet it is a simple truth that only in the eighteenth century did bridges appear in gardens; but this is never (as far as I know) acknowledged.

There are, to be sure, a couple of "possible" bridges in gardens before 1700. One is shown in an engraving of Wilton Gardens,[3] where the central allée of the garden crosses the winding river Nader; that it is a bridge is indicated by what seems to be a shadow of its open balustrade shown on the paving. Another bridge can be found in the gardens of the Paleis Het Loo at Apeldoorn in the Netherlands: the roadway to the Oude Loo (the old castle) crossed the new garden laid out at the end of the seventeenth century, and

46. An "English" garden, as envisaged by the French, with winding paths and three bridges, from G.-L. Le Rouge, *Détails des nouveaux jardins à la mode*, c. 1776–87.

as this new space extends beyond the old road and its neighboring streamlet, it is therefore crossed by two tiny bridges. But no bridges that I can find in Italian or French gardens like Versailles, Vaux, or Villa d'Este; Villa Lante has passageways across to the central island of its water parterre (which I suppose might count as bridges), and there were other, similar bridges, much earlier, at Hadrian's Villa, presumably ones that could be drawn up to provide privacy within the so-called Maritime Theatre for the emperor; the same system was copied, probably, for the Isoletta in the Boboli Gardens. But bridges in gardens were, till the eighteenth century, an absent, or at least meaningless, item.

But during the eighteenth century, bridges proliferated. And they took any number of marvelous and absurd forms and decorations. We can see this in pattern books or collections of fabriques and follies published then and later, in the nineteenth century. So the issue is—why that sudden insertion of bridges in landscape gardens? The answer has two parts: one is formal, a response to other moves in landscape design; the other addresses what those contemporary commentators claimed for the significance of bridges in the new landscapes.

The formal move is actually very simple. The invention of what we like to call "English" or later "picturesque" gardens meant the incidence of winding streams and inlets of lakes or ponds that in their turn intersected with equally winding paths and carriageways; earlier the regular basins or bodies of water might be surrounded with pathways, but these did not cross the water. When path and water encountered each other in these picturesque landscapes, the bridge became a necessity (Figure 46). And what was necessary also became an excuse for formal invention, hence the proliferation of bridges of every description—bridges in different materials (iron or wood), Chinese bridges, Gothic, or rustic items suitable for an English picturesque. There were other exotic types in Germany, like the Devil's Bridge at Kassel-Wilhelmshöhe or the far more functional crossings over streams or bodies of water in the landscape of Hafod in Wales. Many of these designs aped Chinese elements, and they helped to sustain the whole argument that the new garden was (in French eyes at least) the *jardin anglo-chinois*: the Chinese influence came in great part because so many images of eighteenth-century Chinese gardens showed lakes and streams and utilized bridges; we knew of this in Europe through the engravings by the Jesuit Matteo Ripa, whose engravings of Chinese sites Lord Burlington bought in the 1710s.

Some of this fashion was absolutely crazy, but the absurdity helps me to make the more useful point about their possible significance. Bridges therefore entered into the vocabulary of design when so-called informal or picturesque layout predominated. We can see this still today at the Getty Center in Los Angeles, which seems to utilize this particular motif. On the southern edge of Richard Meier's "Tuscan hillside"–like campus, it was decreed that Robert Irwin construct a garden rather different from that previously laid out on the Getty campus by the Olin Studio. Irwin had no experience of garden making, and after purchasing hundreds of flower catalogues, he cut them up to contrive his horticultural profusion and then dumped building materials onto the hillside from which to construct his installation; this was (as he said) to "compose a painting, a little more complicated maybe," presumably because *his* "painting" somehow echoed the paintings held in the Getty Museum; so perhaps a new picturesque.[4] There is a variety of strange references here, including a sort of *chadar* common in Mughal gardens, out of which the stream descends to the lower level, a labyrinth on that level that nobody can enter except gardeners, and bridges over the stream. But what neither Irwin nor his commentators register is his debt to a common feature of picturesque gardens, namely, bridges.

The descent from the main level at the Getty had to be handicap accessible, so Irwin was forced to scrap steps and somewhat awkwardly make a zigzag pathway, which on five occasions has to cross a rather implausible, naturalistic stream, the waters of which descend from the chadar. He said of this motif, "One of the things I wanted to do is that every time you cross the stream, I wanted it to be different, even though it is the same set of elements. But I didn't want you to necessarily be conscious of it. [Rock, water and plants] change at every crossing of the bridge, they're different." (Figure 47).[5] Yet it *is* precisely the differences in the stream that we need to observe (even though we are told not to be conscious of them) rather than the bridges, which are monotonously similar, a fact that maybe helps the visitor to focus on the various elements of the water channel. We get the experience, perhaps, but we miss the meaning (as T. S. Eliot says in the *Four Quartets*).

Beyond the cluster of bridge decorations and devices that emerged during the eighteenth century, bridges were also annexed to some intriguing ideas. One of the most prominent and clearly adumbrated expositions of this significance for bridges came in Claude-Henri Watelet's *Essai sur les jardins*, pub-

47. Irwin's bridges in his garden at the Getty Center, Los Angeles. Photograph by Emily T. Cooperman.

lished in 1774. A motif of Watelet's essay is the explicit connection of friendship and gardens. Friendship was a leitmotif encountered endlessly across Europe, especially when this theme played such a leading role in sentimental thinking throughout Europe in the later eighteenth century, when a work like Lawrence Sterne's *Sentimental Journey* or Rousseau's *Les Rêveries du promeneur solitaire* was widely read. The theme of friendship, for example, can be found in the friendly alliance of Whig politicians (Stowe's Temple of Friendship), a "Field of Friendship" created by Joseph Spence at his estate at Byfleet, benches dedicated to his friends by William Shenstone at The Leasowes, something that Finlay himself took up especially for The Leasowes, where he proposed a similar, inscribed, bench there. There was a monument to Gothic Friendship (Gothische Freundschaft) at the Seifersdorfer Tal, near Leipzig, in what was originally called the Grove of Friends; the place was in fact littered with monuments to all sorts of children, muses, and famous poets and noble friends. Wörlitz has its Pantheon dedicated to "the Friends of Nature and Art," and during the 1780s and 1790s the cardinal archbishop of Passau laid out his own Freundenhain (Grove of Friends), a whole estate with different follies and Dutch villages, all depicted in 1792 by the drawing master of the Passau academy, to show the many friendships that were, so to speak, available;[6] its name was later changed in 1889 to Freudenhain (Grove of Joy). These are just a selection of architectural eighteenth-century celebrations of friendship; a host of such effusions have been studied these days in connection with the cult of sentimentality that flourished in Europe.

Watelet, however, actually makes specific a connection of friendship *with bridges* in the final segment of his *Essai*, significantly entitled "Letter to a Friend."[7] The text is actually a description of his own garden along the river Seine, the Moulin Joli. The *Essai* connects "meandering streams," or more accurately the waters of the river and its tributaries, with "the paths [that trace] softly winding curves." Watelet explains further that "the streams that irrigate the pastures intersect or follow paths opening up before me, while simple little bridges, all different in appearance, allow me to cross over" (p. 28). This site encompassed a series of islands in the river and was therefore provided with a series of bridges, which were sketched by, among others, Hubert Robert and Watelet himself. Watelet says that as soon as he purchased the place, "bridges were built" (p. 67), and then paths were laid out to "link the bridges together . . . to share my delight with friends, to take them to visit the location, to convey my impressions to them, and eventually to become, in their company, both the owner and a resident of the place" (p. 67). Scattered inscriptions celebrated friendship, such as "Live but for a few friends" and "To friendship offer your days on earth." Another quasi-bridge or river overlook was inscribed with an inscription that equated the flow of friendship (its sadness or its joys) with the river's movement, and the visitor then moved on to an actual bridge over the water, where friends could gaze in the "truthful mirror" of the river water. Another bridge rose into the treetops, with more seats where friends could commune with their leafy surroundings.

I would argue that Watelet's connection of bridges with friendship, especially the variety of the different bridges (he claims that "friendship delights in details" [p. 68]), along with the fluctuating sadnesses and joys with which Watelet celebrates friendship, links us 250 years later to the "material curve" of Finlay's "ARCH," which for Finlay "is sustained by gravity, as rapture by grief." It is of course a commonplace that arches are sustained by gravity and that good friendship needs (or better, perhaps, endures) both raptures and grievances. But it is more than a coincidence that the proliferation of bridges in the "new" European gardening seems to have borne some extra dimension that linked architectural items to ideas, associations, and moods.

This is (I hope) interesting as far as it goes; I wanted to understand some of the cultural meanings of garden bridges. But that is, probably, not enough. Indeed, it raises the larger and perhaps more interesting issue of *how* meanings become attached to landscapes (I intend to focus on landscape, though I suspect it can be extended in part to architecture; this theme could obviously be followed by considering a variety of different landscape insertions and elements, though I shall focus here on bridges). If we review the materials discussed above, we can see that between Stowe's Temple of Friendship and Finlay's arch at Little Sparta there is a considerable shift in how meanings attached themselves to places. This shift relates to other essays in this volume on the late eighteenth-century shift from emblems to expressions, as announced by one garden commentator, Thomas Whately, in 1770.[8]

If we return to the Temple of Friendship at Stowe and compare it with both Watelet's interest in friendship at the Moulin Joli some fifty years later and Finlay's bridge in the 2000s, we are clearly confronted with a change in attitudes as to how we respond to a material effect. James Gibbs identified the Stowe temple on its lintel with a Latin dedication to friendship, and the central room inside contained busts of members of the political faction supporting the Prince of Wales against the king and Sir Robert Walpole; frescoes decorated the walls with emblems of Friendship, Justice, and Liberty . . . and so on.[9] It is a fairly explicit plea for the temple's meaning. That we probably need to be educated in its emblematic significance today alerts us to a change in how we receive such work, but the original thrust was clear. The temple did not lend itself readily to alternative readings.

By contrast, while Watelet still uses inscriptions and mottoes around his garden at Moulin Joli, they are both personal (not political) and unspecific—

any visitor who hoped for Watelet's friendship and affection would understand them and be comfortable there. The site itself offered a variety of experiences and effects that subdued or diminished any explicit insistence on one specific meaning and instead celebrated a general, feel-good sense. It recalls Irwin's point about the Getty garden that the visitor is "not conscious" of the significance of the stream that you cross five times, even though it's obviously there.

If we now compare Watelet with Finlay, a further contrast emerges. It is not sentimental in the fashion of the late eighteenth century, though something more akin to the emblematic devices at Stowe. Finlay acknowledges the engineering of the architectural item—the material of the arch is sustained by gravity; when we have seen and appreciated that fact, a parallel is then posited—that the arch is like rapture sustained by grief. (If you're not an engineer or architect, the human parallel might even also help you understand the fact of how the bridge performs.) Finlay's frequent habit of placing inscriptions in his gardens (and indeed on almost all of his other installations), though often—as here—with a much more gnomic color, allows us to respond to the bridge. In this instance, Finlay offers simply a simile: the verbal conjunction "as" (or "like") make clear that the analogy is precisely that, and, since analogies do not prove anything, nobody is confounding an arch with human feelings. It is not sentimental in the mode of Watelet, and it makes (if we wish to attend to it) a fairly precise gloss upon the issue of friendship; the item and the location are precise, as is Finlay's emblematic injunction.

Watelet asks his friends to appreciate how the site he has purchased and cultivated can sustain their affections, but he is not saying that friendship is inherent in the site or its bridges; nothing derives from anything inherent in the place. In fact, Watelet flirts with, but evades, what John Ruskin would strongly object to in 1865: what he called the "pathetic fallacy," through which I must take a small detour.[10] It was the term Ruskin invented to protest against the secular sentimentalism of his age where poets and painters would credit nature with the feelings of human beings. Nothing was ever simple in Ruskin, and (like the devil with Holy Scripture) we can probably find anything we want in his writings: but he identified this fallacy as "an excited state of the feelings, making us, for the time, more or less irrational"; or, an "error . . . which the mind admits when affected strongly by emotion."[11] Ruskin always decried the interference of "emotion" and its detrimental effects on language or painting (and let's face it, also on his marriage).

Yet Ruskin's preamble to this same chapter makes a rather different point (and this is the endless problem with Ruskin, as he shifts his ground and argues his way along without often stopping to see how he has changed his ideas along the way.) He very properly refuses any false and absolute distinction between "objective" and "subjective": or rather, he wants us to see that a thing has a certain ontology, it does this or that, but not under a misconceived "influence of emotion, or contemplative fancy." He is nothing if not focused on this theme; it was an unending emphasis, on seeing and depicting objects precisely, or on what he calls "the pure fact." This was similar to what Gerard Manley Hopkins would later call "the plain and leafy fact" when he insisted, following Duns Scotus, on the intrinsic being of everything. Ruskin emphasizes this same insistence on pure fact everywhere—in drawing, in verbal descriptions, in discussing paintings by the Pre-Raphaelites or Turner: a person, he says, may "perceive rightly *in spite of his feelings*," with the result that "if we can see that if the feeling is true, we pardon, or are even pleased by the confessed fallacy of sight which it induces." So Ruskin allows an escape through a proper and unbending attention to what we see, and *thereafter* acknowledges some influence of emotion. I think we may see Finlay's remark on his bridge in a similar light—the arch is *rightly perceived for its material effect* yet endorses an affective "fallacy of sight."

Ruskin's identification of that fallacy lies, surely, behind the rather neglected book by a crucial architectural writer, Geoffrey Scott's *Architecture of Humanism*, which appeared in 1914 (and again in 1924).[12] Scott inveighs against a whole host of "fallacies" that have cluttered the proper appreciation of Renaissance and baroque architecture—there is the romantic fallacy (picturesque and naturalism), the mechanical and ethical fallacies, the biological and the academic or literary fallacies. What I need to pull out here is his obvious allusion to Ruskin's "pathetic fallacy" when he discusses how we respond to what Scott himself calls, and himself wants to celebrate, the "immediate aspect" of architecture "as it is concerned with appearances" (p. 157). Yet what he argues is curiously like Ruskin's own assent to a certain kind of pathetic fallacy. We read architecture, Scott writes, "in terms of ourselves": a spire soars, arches spring, domes swell, and so on. "The whole of architecture is, in fact, unconsciously invested by us with a human movement and human moods" (p. 159). It is, Scott says, a metaphor, an "unconscious analogy" between ourselves and the forms of the exterior world. He seems to echo Ruskin in saying that this "poetic mind in all times and places, which humanized the external world" is premised upon "*perceiving*" it rightly, and not through a "series of artificial conceits" (p. 162).

This final chapter of Scott's book, entitled "Humanist Values," is dense and is at the center of the his argument; it can be useful to read it as his final positive response to his earlier identification of fallacies, though I have no time to take you through it (I suggest, though, that you read it first, without pushing through his catalogue of fallacies, which are somewhat ambiguous).[13] Scott's ideas are almost entirely focused on architecture, not landscape architecture: the central aspects or elements of architecture he calls "space, mass, line and coherence" (p. 186); yet some of these may yet be transferred to landscape. He writes that "space, in fact, is liberty of movement" (p. 166), and in acknowledging "voids" (as opposed to solids) he addresses indirectly the world of landscape where voids as well as specific objects constitute its essence.[14] Scott connects motion with emotion in his discussion: "The architect . . . in the lines of a design . . . controls the path of the eye; the path we follow [with our eye] is our movement; movement determines our mood" (p. 166). That seems to me to describe exactly Finlay's bridges. Scott argues—again I think with a glance at Ruskin—that while science offers an "intelligent system" to understand nature, the "groups which the eye, at any one glance, discovers in Nature are not intelligible" and are only opened to our attention by memory and by imagination of "things not actually seen" (p. 176).

We are here, surely, in a world where empathy,[15] association, emotion, and significance rule (I prefer "significance" to "meaning," as I explained in my discussion of Stourhead gardens in Chapter 3).[16] Scott is specifically attentive to the issue of empathy, even though he does not specifically tout that term. So I come, as I am forced to do, to Heidegger on bridges. I don't want to, but his remarks help me elucidate how we may tackle this aspect of landscape that deals with significance. Harry Gilonis reminded us that Finlay's glass bridge in Provence (Figure 48) may refer us to Heidegger's discussion of a bridge in "Building Dwelling Thinking," and Gilonis says, "Bridge-crossings prefigure our own final journeys." But that is not quite what Heidegger says, nor is it particularly apt to nourish that association in Provence.[17]

Heidegger affirms that a bridge "gathers the earth as landscape around it," and that "a location comes into existence only by virtue of the bridge."[18] (That is also surely true of other insertions in landscape besides bridges. I think this

48. Fleur de l'Air, Provence, glass bridge at the bottom of the gardens. Photograph by Emily T. Cooperman.

can also be true of stiles, of which Finlay is exceptionally fond and which he utilizes also in Provence, and on which his inscriptions take us beyond the form and utility of stiles. But I'll stick to bridges.) Without Finlay's bridges, then, the landscape in Provence or Little Sparta would be less defined and less visible; we see it more clearly because of the careful insertion of the bridge into that particular landscape;[19] the area at Little Sparta—the last to be designed before Finlay's death—is an "English Parkland," a relaxed and unbusy mead-ow where Finlay's bridge, with its striking and stiff form, is more conspicuous in itself and for what it performs in this particular area. The bridge at Little Sparta, like that in the rough wilderness in Provence, formulates, or gives form to, a location within areas that are far less focused and coherent; so the bridge gathers the landscape around it.

Heidegger continues his commentary on bridges by saying, "The bridge is a location. As such a thing, it allows a space into which earth and heaven, divinities and mortals are admitted" (p. 331) and later, "The relationship between man and space is none other than dwelling, thought essentially" (p. 335). Essentially *thought*. Now that is a grand if not grandiloquent remark, not least because it moves us, beyond anything as tangible or objective as a bridge, into a virtually mystical world. Maybe I am too touched by positivism or perhaps empiricism to find that general claim very useful. I have several concerns, besides wanting to attach significance to something precise: does that mean that *any thought* can be admitted? *Quot homines, tot sententiae*? Does *any thought* whatsoever enable that sufficient *dwelling*? Surely the answer must be no, for that would mean any thought would be as valuable or as useless as any other. This would place an almost total reliance on individual reception: while I have long been fascinated by the role of reception in viewing landscape, what I take to be Heidegger's remark on thought eludes any understanding I have of how reception should work in assisting our understanding of place, both in its original formulation and its subsequent evolution. On the one hand, a designer today cannot *dictate* or even allow a context in which ideas and associations *are certain* to be found; equally, no visitors can automatically attribute what they find in a place to the *intentions* of a designer in the first place. So a site hovers between a designer's intention and the fulfillment of it by a visitor.

Now Finlay's bridges, as indeed much of his other work, work in different ways—but as a designer he directs a response through his inscriptions; we may not buy it, but his intent is at least made poetically available. In his three bridges, he makes clear how he would wish us to view them—besides being bridges that shape their locations, they also provoke our ideas, and he always does this in a context that allows us to see its specificity in that instance. It is, in a Hopkinsian way, the plain and leafy fact of a thing first of all.

Now when in *The Ethical Function of Architecture* Karsten Harries discusses Heidegger's bridges, he seeks to explain Heidegger's remarks by reminding us of the specific occasion of their delivery to a group of German architects in 1951 in the wake of a severe housing shortage after World War II. Now I am not competent to understand that context fully, but it does suggest—and I like Harries's book a lot—that *how* and *when* something is said will depend upon the circumstances, even when—as here—it is hugely generalized. The generalization presumably worked at the German conference, had a certain resonance, at that particular juncture, even if it now floats uneasily without one.

I expect and look for meaning in things of all sorts. There is a move in current design that downplays meaning; Marc Treib wants to confine his analyses to form and formal matters and is skeptical about all claims for meaning.[20] I cannot understand this refusal to accept the humanist attachment to landscape: it is never a merely formal affair, and humans are always involved. On the other hand, I am wary—obviously—about imposing any meaning upon a design; I accept historical understandings, as with the temples at Stowe in the mid-eighteenth century, but also I think that the afterlife of these places acquires a patina and a significance that, while unhistorical, can augment our understanding of them. In the end I need to annex significance to specific places in specific circumstances, and these circumstances will undoubtedly change over time. And also change over place—I do not see that bridges anywhere and everywhere bear the same meaning. Like Scott, I am wary of literary fallacies, where "signs" can only be read as "a sign of intervention";[21] like Scott, architecture and landscape architecture are experienced sensuously in substance and form, but those are not the end of the matter. I am interested in what one thing at one time and place is doing and appears to be saying, and appears to be saying in ways that bear interpretation by visitors (there is no word to deal with this experience—maybe "spectatorship" might serve).[22] Sometimes it can be clear that a site acquires its significance from properties inherent in it—like a bridge. But human minds also do bestow, if they so feel, affections on a place.

Afterword

From Literature to Landscape

The route from being a critic of literature to being a commentator on landscape gardening is probably not obvious. Yet I managed to follow that career path by a happy collusion between the happenstance of my teaching and research and my own impulse to—somehow—relate what was written to what was seen. So I eventually jumped ship into garden and landscape studies, yet without totally losing my sense of what my literary training had taught me about the word.

I AM OFTEN asked how someone trained in literary studies could end up in landscape architecture. Generally, I have a simple reply, but the more complicated one is, I think, interesting. When I arrived back in England in 1962 (after three years of teaching English literature in the United States), I landed a job in the Department of English at the University of Exeter, where (as was customary then) I was told by the professor what I was to lecture on: my course was to be on eighteenth-century poetry, which I must confess was not then a topic about which I was excited. But chores are chores, and I settled into the task, focusing first on the poetry of Alexander Pope. In reading his work—more than I had done as an undergraduate—I discovered what Pope himself called his "gardening poem." It was actually one of Pope's *Moral Essays,* addressed to Lord Burlington. But the poem contained a passage on the gardens of Stowe. Never having heard of them, I looked them up, found that they were the grounds of a public (that is, private, in U.S. terms) school, which I did know. So I decided to visit.

The gardens were extensive, and with a basic map that the school office had given me, I started to explore. During my walk I encountered one of the schoolmasters, who asked what I was doing, so I explained that I was trying to see how Pope's lines on Stowe could be construed. The master turned out to be George Clarke, who actually taught an O level course on landscape architectural history (probably the only course offered on that subject in the whole of the United Kingdom!). He was himself an accomplished historian of the gardens, and he invited me to come back and see the gardens again. When I did, he took me round, using his copy of William Gilpin's *Dialogue upon the Gardens . . . at Stow*, a photocopy of which he gave me. And this text I later edited for the Augustan Reprint Society in 1976.

I was hooked. Partly, I had always been interested in nonliterary arts, and spent more time going to lectures on art and architecture at Cambridge than to literary ones (Nikolaus Pevsner, Michael Jaffe, and Francis Haskell were all lecturing in art and architectural history during my time there). After Cambridge, I did a Ph.D. on the Pre-Raphaelites—as writers, but I was drawn into asking what Rossetti's women were doing in his paintings as well as in poems like "The Blessed Damosel," and that gave me the chance to write a chapter on the iconography of "the Pre-Raphaelite woman." It was not, it must be confessed, any good as art history, and I was told so by David Piper in an otherwise kind review of my eventual book *The Pre-Raphaelite Imagination*. But I had found my way, if poorly and sideways, into art history. And once the Ph.D. was done and heading to publication, I wanted to work on John Ruskin, whom I realized was explicitly involved with both the word and the image. Yet at that point, when modern Ruskin studies had not yet taken off, there came a brilliant book, *The Darkening Glass: A Portrait of Ruskin's Genius*, by John D. Rosenberg (1963), and I realized that this was the sort of book I would have tried to write; so I stayed away (at least then) from Ruskin. I became interested, *faute de mieux*, in writings on and about the making of gardens.

For some twenty years I kept up my work in both literature and art and design, by exploring poems about paintings, writing about gardens (Andrew Marvell, Jane Austen, and William Gilpin), and penning some essays on landscape painting. And I planned to complete a book on Shakespeare and the paragone, namely, the dialogue of the seen and the spoken in his plays. That would probably have satisfied my literature colleagues, who (I suspect) eyed with some misgiving my "dabbling" in nonliterary topics. But on the other hand, I was beginning to be dismayed by the fashion in which literary study was focusing more and more on theoretical issues that largely removed readers from any focus on and discussion of actual texts. I didn't want to go that way and, as it happened, a focus on "texts," that is to say, what I saw in gardens and landscapes, became my particular concern when I moved finally into work on landscape.

That chance came in 1988 from an invitation to replace Elisabeth Mac-Dougall, a distinguished art and garden historian, as director of studies in landscape at Dumbarton Oaks in Washington, D.C. I had by then written three books on landscape topics and was editing the *Journal of Garden History* (later called *Studies in the History of Gardens and Designed Landscapes*), which I had been asked to edit by Taylor and Francis in the wake of the garden exhibition that took place at the Victoria and Albert Museum in 1980, curated by Roy Strong and John Harris. Landscape studies in the United States had largely risen from art historical approaches—like MacDougall's or David Coffin's—but I was interested in what could be said about landscape architecture from other, non-art-historical perspectives that might engage that material. At the same time, I wanted to get to know the work of, and talk to, practicing landscape architects, and I started a series of informal discussion groups at Dumbarton Oaks where these ideas would be aired.

It has always seemed to me that the way I was trained in literature both at my English grammar school and at Cambridge could be transferred to a study of landscape: namely, to absorb myself in the "text" (that is, the site), practice upon it what was in literary studies called "practical criticism," and seek to probe the fullest meanings of sites, yet doing so within (or sustained by) a proper inquiry into a site's historical and cultural contexts. Furthermore, as a student of literature and, later, as a university teacher of English, I'd was required to know the whole of the subject (whatever specialization I preached in my publications); so it was inevitable that I wanted to explore the full narrative of gardens and landscapes (at that point only in Western culture, though I have since acquired some small understanding of non-European oriental garden work).

I also wondered whether I should retrain as a landscape architect. But that ambition was nipped in the bud at a conference of the International Federation of Landscape Architects in the Netherlands in 1992, an event where a cluster of great names spoke on the "interface" between landscape architecture and the visual arts—Bernard Lassus, Georges Descombes, Martha Schwartz, Lucius Burckhardt, among others. In the course of responding to a question from the audience, I said that I thought I should perhaps become a landscape architect; but a voice from the rear of the hall said (something like) "No, no; go on doing what you do." The voice came up to me afterward, and I met Peter Walker, and I have tried ever since then to "do what I was doing." His example, like those of many other landscape architects (in particular, Bernard Lassus, Peter Latz, and Paolo Bürgi), have sustained my explorations ever since.

But I also found that, even if I didn't want to retrain, I still needed to know much more about what had been written in the past about landscape architecture, and that opportunity came when I worked for three years at the Oak Spring Garden Library in Virginia, where Rachel Mellon had gathered a rich collection of books, drawings, plans, and other responses to gardens and landscapes from the early Renaissance onward. In that handsome building and among her treasures, I read and then catalogued everything in that collection that addressed garden design, with sections dedicated to the landscape histories of different nations—those of the United States, Great Britain, France, Italy, the Netherlands, Germany, and Scandinavia. It was a hugely rewarding time, and I amassed a wide-ranging knowledge of what had been written on garden design and criticism for more than six centuries across Europe and America.

That immense research completed, I was lucky—not to retrain as a landscape architect but—to be appointed chair of the Department of Landscape Architecture at the University of Pennsylvania, in which capacity I served for six years. The department was famous for its previous chairs, Ian McHarg and Anne Whiston Spirn, and those who taught there as well as all the studio critics and visitors offered me a new education in relating my historical inquiries to the world of the young landscape architects whom we were training.

These professional stimuli and moves were matched in a series of publications. I had begun writing about landscape in relation to literature, or what sprang out of that initial visit to Stowe in 1963, in my book *The Figure in the Landscape: Poetry, Painting and Gardening in the Eighteenth Century* (1976). But I still wanted to find out where the eighteenth-century landscape had come from, and that took me into material much less focused now on literary resources: *The Genius of the Place: The English Landscape Garden 1620–1820*

(1975), a collection of writings on English garden design and practice coedited with Peter Willis; then *Garden and Grove: The Italian Renaissance Garden in the English Imagination: 1600–1750* (1986) and *William Kent: Landscape Garden Architect: An Assessment and Catalogue Raisonné* (1987). If those last two books allowed me to break free from much reliance on literary materials, I was still tempted by the exchange between writing and looking at places, and this led me to a collection of essays, *Gardens and the Picturesque: Studies in the History of Landscape Architecture* (1992), and ten years later *The Picturesque Garden in Europe* (2002). But I also was much engaged in editing a journal, *Word & Image: A Journal of Verbal-Visual Enquiry,* that I had proposed to the publishers, who were, once again, Taylor and Francis.

But teaching landscape architecture students made it almost inevitable that I would realize that what the field seemed to need was some theoretical discussion of its scope and history. Hence I worked to draw out of my readings and landscape visits a sense of the principles that had sustained—and might continue to be useful to—landscape architecture. So I tried out some conceptual approaches (a term I prefer to theoretical) in two lectures delivered at the Collège de France and published in Paris as *L'art du jardin et son histoire* (Travaux du Collège de France) in 1996. And, emboldened by some European responses to those talks, in 2000 I published *Greater Perfections: The Practice of Garden Theory* (a subtitle suggested by my colleague David Leatherbarrow). I was amused to be drawn into the realm of theory—especially after I'd fled what I took to be its excessive grip on literary studies—but my excuse was that I needed to elicit from the actual work and writings of landscapists some conceptual basis for what they did.

From that point I have moved increasing to study and write about modern and contemporary gardens and landscapes, based to be sure upon what I conceived as the long narrative of those arts of place making that I sketched in *A World of Gardens* (2012). So these were an inquiry into how gardens have been received (rather than how they were designed), which I called *The Afterlife of Gardens* (2004); a study of the garden art of Ian Hamilton Finlay (*Nature Over Again,* 2008); a collection of essays on the modern period for the six-volume *Cultural History of Gardens*, the whole series coedited with a friend, Michael Leslie (2012); and most recently in 2014 an exploration of how contemporary landscape designers have used or invented ("feigned") history when designing sites, a book called *Historical Ground.*

I do not think that I have ever lost sight of what I had been taught (and tried to practice) as a literary critic—that the text/site itself should lead my analyses and sustain whatever conceptual ideas can be drawn from those local examples. Nor have I lost the habit and the need to try to write about landscape architecture for an audience outside the professional field, so that—unflummoxed by jargon and in-house design speak—they could be tempted into the field to which I so happily had gravitated. I try to bear in mind the lesson of Isaac Newton: he once thought to write his *Principia* in *methodo populari* (that is, in the vernacular) to ensure that it would be widely read; in the end he wrote in deadly Latin thickened with theorems and propositions. His earlier ambition for mathematics still pertains to landscape.

Notes

Chapter 1. The *Lie* of the Land

1   I made a first stab at this topic in a lecture in Nanjing, subsequently published as "Topography, History and the Lie of the Land," in *Architectural Studies*, no. 2, issue entitled "Topography and Mental Space," ed. Mark Cousins et al. (China Architecture and Building Press, 2012), pp. 43–71. In English and in Chinese. This is a topic that I pursued in *Historical Ground* (London: Routledge, 2014).

2   "It is all too easy to imagine perfectly clean environments that are not attractive at all. By contrast, it is quite possible to appreciate landscapes that, from the environmental point of view, leave a lot to be desired." Bernard Lassus, *The Landscape Approach of Bernard Lassus* (Philadelphia: University of Pennsylvania Press, 1998), p. 80.

3   See Joseph Disponzio, "Jean-Marie Morel and the Invention of Landscape Architecture," in *Tradition and Innovation in French Garden Art*, ed. John Dixon Hunt and Michel Conan (Philadelphia: University of Pennsylvania Press, 2002), pp. 137–59; quotations from pp. 135 and 139. Morel's book, *Théorie des jardins*, published in 1776, with a second edition in 1802, has never been translated, but the author's command of both natural sciences and their application to topography make him a pioneer in *ecological* assessment of landscape (though he never used the word).

4   J. B. Jackson, *The Necessity of Ruins* (Amherst: University of Massachusetts Press, 1980), p. 3.

5   I have discussed this analogy more fully in *Historical Ground*, chapter 1.

6   This is my own phrase, but strangely similar to the Chinese injunction, for which I am indebted to my graduate student at Harvard, Michael Lee, and, for his elucidation of it, to Derek Gilman, who writes to me: "Guan 观 is simply to see; xiang 想 is the slightly ambiguous term here. My sense is that together they capture the idea of thinking visually but not mimetically. Perhaps more (but still not quite there): Site, Sight, Farsight."

7   This a topic taken up by such aestheticians as Cheryl Foster, in "The Narrative and the Ambient in Environmental Aesthetcis," *Journal of Aesthetics and Art Criticism* 56, no. 2 (1998), pp. 127–37. I discussed this in different ways in a talk that I gave at a Dumbarton Oaks symposium in May 2014 on the role of scents and sounds in a garden or landscape.

8   Beth Meyer, "The Expanded Field of Landscape Architecture," in *Ecological*

Design and Planning, ed. George Thompson and Frederick Steiner (New York: Wiley, 1997), pp. 45–97.

9   One might also adduce the work of Roman Jakobson and his insistence on the "poetic lie," a "lie" that sustains the heart of poetry ("What Is Poetry?"), something good in itself without needing to referring to "reality."

10   Paolo Bürgi, *Field Studies: The New Aesthetics of Urban Agriculture* (Basel: Birkhauser, 2010).

11   Denis Cosgrove, *Social Formation and Symbolic Landscape* (London: Croom Helm, 1984), p. 13.

12   For a more thorough description of Adam's work see: Lewis Baltz, *Lewis Baltz Texts* (Göttingen: Steidl, 2012), pp. 33–37. To place Adam's work within the history of landscape photography, and for more on the importance of the New Topographics Movement, see Greg Foster-Rice and John Rohrbach, eds., *Reframing the New Topographics* (Chicago: University of Chicago Press, 2013). I was introduced to these ideas by Matt Damon.

Chapter 2. Near and Far, and the Spaces in Between

1   *Landschaftsmalerei von Brughel bis Corinth,* ed. Bastian Eclercy (Hanover: Wienand, 2011). The museum owns a considerable collection of Netherlandish paintings, so it was a good occasion on which to feature them in this way.

2   It should be noted, however, that paintings in other cultures—medieval and Asian—also neglected the perspectival format.

3   Some indication of Lassus's formation as a painter is set out by Stephen Bann, *Le destin paysager de Bernard Lassus / Bernard Lassus, The Landscape Approach* (Orleans: Éditions HYX, 2014), a bilingual text.

4   This remark, by a well-known landscape practitioner and critic, is a familiar lament, so, as it has general application, it seems unnecessary to pillory one writer over others who think the same.

5   It is possible that viewers of earlier paintings, such as those by Giorgione or Veronese, also thought they might explore those represented landscapes, but it is—to my knowledge—Diderot who activated promoted this idea and explained in his prose how it could work.

6   Quoted by Ian J. Lochhead, *The Spectator and the Landscape in the Art Criticism of Diderot and His Contemporaries* (Ann Arbor: UMI Research Press, 1982), p. 47. See also Denis Diderot, *Essais sur la peinture [et] Salons de 1759, 1761, 1763,* ed. Jacques Chouillet (Paris: Hermann, 1984), and *Diderot et l'art de Boucher à David,* catalogue by various authors (Paris: Éditions de la Réunion des Musées nationaux, 1984).

7   Yves Abrioux, "Near and Far," in *Ian Hamilton Finlay: A Visual Primer,* 2nd ed. (London: Reaktion Books, 1992), p. 167, and for the concrete poem cited below, p. 173.

8   Ian Hamilton Finlay, *Selected Ponds,* with an introduction by Bernard Lassus (Reno, Nev.: West Coast Poetry Review, 1976), unpaginated.

9   Bernard Lassus, *The Landscape Approach* (Philadelphia: University of Penn-

sylvania Press, 1998), p. 43. Other quotations from this collection of his writings or from commentary in that volume by other commentators are cited in the text.

10   Ibid., p. 6. I do not mean to be too categorical in distinguishing between Lassus's tactile and visual: everything we can touch nearby is also a visual experience, but (I would suggest) that the visual is here different from the tactile.

11   Lassus illustrates his essay with a series of photographs that make clear his changing perceptions as he moves through the harbor area: ibid., pp. 24–25. He also discusses this phenomenon in his "Theory of Faults," ibid., pp. 62–63.

12   I owe this observation to David Leatherbarrow, whose comments on an early draft of this essay much improved it.

13   One of the most accomplished photographers of landscape is the Canadian Geoffrey James, and his use of a 1920s Eastman Kodak allows us the luxury of looking in different directions as his apparatus surveys the scene; smartphones are also now able to take wide-angle views. Geoffrey James, *Genius Loci* (Ottawa: Canadian Museum of Contemporary Photography, 1986).

14   Northrop Frye writing about Shakespeare's *The Winter's Tale* in *Writings on Shakespeare and the Renaissance*, ed. Troni Grande and Garry Sherbert (Toronto: University of Toronto Press, 2010), p. 199.

15   Quoted by Finlay in his interview with Udo Weilacher, in *Between Landscape Architecture and Land Art* (Berlin: Birkhauser, 1996), p. 102

16   Matsuo Basho (trans. N. Yuasa), a seventeenth-century poet.

17   G. W. F. Hegel, "Naturphilosophie," trans. Terry Pinkard, in *Continental Philosophy of Science*, ed. Gary Gutting (Oxford: Blackwell, 2005), p. 36.

18   Cited by James Elkins, "The Coherence of Garden Writing," in *Our Beautiful, Dry and Distant Texts: Art History As Writing* (University Park: Pennsylvania State University Press, 1997), p. 271.

19   "Mastered' is the word used by Wallace Stevens when, in his poem "An Idea of Order at Key West," he negotiates between the here and now (the sound of a song) and the far ocean and its boats in the harbor.

20   Richard B. Pilgrim, "Intervals ('Ma') in Space and Time: Foundations for a Religious-Aesthetic Paradigm in Japan," *History of Religions* 25, no. 3 (1986), 255–77. I owe this reference to Nuith Morales, who outlined these ideas in an essay written for a course at Harvard's Graduate School of Design in 2012.

21   Perhaps a way of thinking of landscape experience is to, again, take a "picturesque" stance and look to how painters like Turner understood and painted the sun: see Ronald Paulson's discussion of the sun as a "Revolutionary Aspect" (and a revelatory one) in *Literary Landscape: Turner and Constable* (New Haven: Yale University Press, 1982), pp. 80–98.

Chapter 3. Stourhead Revisited and the Pursuit of Meaning in Gardens

1   Some of these discussions have been conducted by philosophers, whose business is with the way we think rather than the actual being or character of a garden *per se*. See Appendix 2 for a list that includes them.

2   For a Stourhead bibliography see Appendix 1; titles will be referenced within the text, This mode of referencing might be cumbersome, but it is crucial, since we need to track precise statements as we review them. Most of these articles use extensive illustrations to sustain their arguments, so in my own essay I have introduced just a few images relevant to my own discussion.

3   It is immaterial to this discussion whether that body of water was "rectangular" (Turner 1979, p. 68); but the drawing does not to my eyes make that a certainty.

4   Woodbridge (1974) wavers between claiming that he proposed an "iconographical programme based on *The Aeneid*" and then later in the same short article saying that as the garden grew in stages it did not have an iconographical program "from the start."

5   I am thinking of David R. Coffin, *The Villa D'Este at Tivoli* (Princeton: Princeton University Press, 1960) and *The Villa in the Life of Renaissance Rome* (Princeton: Princeton University Press, 1979), and Elizabeth Blair MacDougall, *Fountains, Statues, and Flowers; Studies in Italian Gardens of the 16th and 17th Centuries* (Washington, D.C.: Dumbarton Oaks, 1994). It is perhaps interesting to note that when Coffin turned his attention to an English eighteenth-century garden like Rousham, the iconographical approach seemed strained and unconvincing: see *The English Garden: Meditation and Memorial* (Princeton: Princeton University Press 1994).

6   Thus Paulson at the Temple of Flora/Ceres, having quoted its Virgilian inscription, tells us how the poem continues at that point (1975, p. 29).

7   There have been attempts to assess this quality or character: see my own chapter "What Is a Garden?" in *Greater Perfections: The Practice of Garden Theory* (Philadelphia: University of Pennsylvania Press, and London: Thames & Hudson, 2000) and more recently David E. Cooper, *A Philosophy of Gardens* (Oxford: Oxford University Press, 2006).

8   Here it seems relevant to invoke my discussion in Chapter 2 of the places in between that do not include any iconographical objects yet are also part of the garden experience.

9   True, Charlesworth also avers: "I do not necessarily require an explanation to embrace all the structures of a garden" (2003, p. 268), though he seems in effect to do just the opposite.

10   Gillette is an odd exception here, in that she wishes to reserve meaning in gardens *only* for those actually in novels and denies it wholly to real or actual ones.

11   Charlesworth does note that "different interpretations can be sustained about a garden that developed throughout several decades" (2003, p. 268); however, he does not take that insight further. Turner, by contrast, is interested in the early physical development of the Stourhead complex.

12   It was Sir Richard Colt Hoare, in the third generation, who laid out the gravel path around the lake and who wrote in his "memoirs," "We must keep to the right-hand walk, which will lead us to a small Temple with a Doric portico" (quoted Malins 1966, p. 54). Whether that is the same thing as saying that Colt Hoare "introduced" the route of the circuit walk now followed (Turner 1979, p. 71) is not certain.

13   Paulson (1975, p. 30) curiously attributes "alternative paths" to the design of

Stourhead, a phenomenon that better describes other eighteenth-century designs like Rousham; instead, though, he describes Hoare's "pictorial circuit."

14   Probably novels at least are "read" or reviewed in the mind of a given reader in such a fashion, as he or she traces various "routes" through its plot, scenes, and characters; a painting, too, does not yield itself wholly to an "instant" review but allows different eyes to travel across it in different ways. As Michael Leslie points out to me, Kelsall's scrutiny of the Claude painting, which otherwise he fails to accept as an adequate model for unlocking the meaning of Stourhead, isolates the distant tower, which he then invokes as significant.

15   A letter of Hoare's cited by Woodbridge (1970a, p. 53).

16   It will be noted that Olin as late as 1999 rehearses ideas from Woodbridge that Kelsall had dismissed a few years earlier; reference to Kelsall's corrective work is also missing from Gillette's bibliography.

17   See *The Afterlife of Gardens* (2003), pp. 200–205.

18   But Malins (1966, pp. 49–50) lists many more paintings than are ever considered relevant by modern critics to unlock the garden with paintings, and Horace Walpole himself listed many more at Stourhead than are invoked as keys to the gardens—see *Journals of Visits to Country Seats*, in *Walpole Society Publications* 16 (1928), pp. 41–43. Yet it is typical of the ruts into which analysis gets its wheels stuck that only "Claudean" paintings are deemed relevant (Schulz 1985, p. 22), even though Hoare himself appealed to Gaspar Dughet (see Woodbridge 1970a, p. 53).

19   It is worth noticing that William Hazlitt remarked on the descent into Stourton village "by a sharp winding declivity, almost like going underground between high hedges of laurel trees" (quoted Malins 1966, p. 51). This is exactly how the modern visitor to the National Trust property arrives today.

20   Woodbridge, who was the first to invoke the painting, did not at first make it anything more than a possible inspiration for Henry Hoare himself; it grew later for him and also in others' hands into an obligatory interpretative clue to both Hoare's intentions and our understanding of the garden.

21   Even though based formally upon the Pantheon, the building was designated first as a "Temple of Hercules," and so recognized by Richard Pococke in 1754 (quoted Malins 1966, p. 55).

22   The Swedish visitor Piper marks it on his plan as Flora in 1779, illustrated in color in Sven-Ingvar Andersson et al., *Great European Gardens: An Atlas of Historic Plans* (Copenhagen: Danish Architectural Press, 2006), p. 125.

23   I am indebted to Edward Harwood for suggesting this extension of Charlesworth's interpretation.

24   This is the path that leads beside the stream which feeds the lake at this point and over which we must cross before turning back along the lakeside to find, if we do, the climbing path up to Apollo. Admittedly it is not a particularly likely or inviting path, as the visitor would almost certainly wish to continue around the lake; but it is, nonetheless, the first forking path encountered after seeing the Hercules.

25   "Authorized" would require an author, and it ignores the fact that visiting the lakeside gardens from the house could entail starting the lake circuit at a point

different from where one would begin when arriving via the church (the modern National Trust entrance).

26 For this well-established point see Earl Wasserman, "The Inherent Values of Eighteenth-Century Personification," *PMLA* 65, 435–63 (especially pp. 437–40); there is also the essay "A notion of the historical draught or Tablature of the Judgement of Hercules," written by the widely read Earl of Shaftesbury—see extracts in *A Documentary History of Art*, ed. Elizabeth G. Holt, vol. 2 (New York: Doubleday Anchor, 1947), pp. 242–59. And Charlesworth extends this point by showing how the choice of Hercules enjoyed an extended life into the later nineteenth century (2003, pp. 280ff.)

27 In short, the inscriptions, read in the light of Benveniste's theories, "invite the visitor across a crucial threshold that separates the mythic domain of the garden from the real space" (Charlesworth, p. 285, citing Benveniste's *Problèmes de linguistique générale* of 1966).

28 See Turner 1979, notes 12, 17, 22, 26, 30, and 36.

29 Walpole was actually dead right, since that is what the original sculpture from which the Stourhead nymph was copied does indeed represent (see Elisabeth Blair MacDougall, "The Sleeping Nymph: Origins of a Humanist Fountain Type," in the volume *Fountains, Statues, and Flowers*, cited in note 5, pp. 3756). However, the antiquarian precision shown by Walpole does not help any one interpretation. It should be noted that Malins (1966, p. 52) briefly discussed the origins of the Sleeping Nymph before MacDougall.

30 In this regard, see my use of some collected writings of visitors to Stowe that do not seem to conform to our modern interpretations of its landscape design in *The Afterlife of Gardens* (2003, pp. 121–29).

31 To be fair here to Charlesworth, he does base his new interpretation upon the very salient fact, noted already, that Woodbridge's explanation of meaning essentially stops half way round the lake at the Pantheon, thus neglecting other items still to be encountered.

32 See Woodbridge (1974): "This is conjecture; the records do not tell us." Kelsall's essay did not deter some others—Olin and Gillette, for example—because they missed it.

33 I address the more general issue in *The Cultural History of Gardens*, ed. Michael Leslie and John Dixon Hunt (London: Bloomsbury, 2013), specifically in a chapter entitled "Meaning" in vol. 6, *The Modern Garden*, ed. Hunt. The present essay was by way of clearing the throat for that more daunting enterprise.

34 I have discussed and tried to remove this "intentional fallacy" from the study of designed landscapes: see *The Afterlife of Gardens* (2003, pp. 14–15).

35 True, one can imagine a site being laid out with an explicit itinerary and reenacting or representing of stages in a already well-known narrative, clues to which could be visually or even verbally inserted: the *sacre monte* in northern Italy are just such creations. But short of a Disney-like version of the *Aeneid* we cannot expect a garden to tell Virgil's story.

36 Paulson (1975, pp. 28–30), as pointed out by Schulz (1980, p. 9). Though this association never enters into the Stourhead analyses, Apollo as leader of the Muses was

a frequent presence in earlier gardens: see my "Pegaso in villa: Variazioni sul tema," in *Villa Lante a Bagnaia*, ed. Sabine Frommel (Milan: Electa, 2005), pp. 132–43.

37   *Pace* Charlesworth (2003, p. 268), allusion is by no means a "modern" practice or assumption; we might simply think of that admirable account of eighteenth-century poetry by Reuben Brower in *Alexander Pope: The Poetry of Allusion* (Oxford: Oxford University Press, 1959).

38   I will give references by volume and chapter, here I.1. This is not (alas!) the place in which to pursue in detail the fascinating parallels between Sterne's writing of a novel and its assumptions about a "model reader" (to use Charlesworth's phrase).

39   This is a continuous concern of Sterne's, but see in particular I.21, VIII.32, and IX.20, and my commentary thereon in my inaugural lecture at the University of Leiden, *A Handle on "Tristram Shandy": or, Uncle Toby's Wound and Other Words and Images* (1984).

40   *Letters of Laurence Sterne*, ed. L. P. Curtis (Oxford: Oxford University Press, 1935), p. 411.

41   Gillette wishes to reserve a meaningful role only for gardens in fiction (2005, p. 85), where of course the author controls—*pace* Sterne—everything a reader observes about a site.

42   But Gillette herself misidentifies a drawing of the mansion at Stourhead as "Woburn Abbey" (2005, p. 6) and in describing the content of another sketch cannot count the number of cows.

43   Turner does use a Bamflyte drawing to deduce the shape of an early pond at Stourhead (1979, p. 68).

44   Yve-Alain Bois, "A Picturesque Stroll Around *Clara-Clara*," October 29 (1984), 32–62.

Chapter 4. Thomas Whately's *Observations on Modern Gardening*

1   I have drawn here upon an earlier publication of mine, "Putting You in the Picture: Visual Image and *Ekphrasis* in Publications of the Picturesque Garden," *Die Gartenkunst* 15, no. 2 (2003), 290–97.

2   All quotations are taken from the edition with an introduction by John Dixon Hunt (New York: Ursus. 1995).

3   Jane Gillette, "Can Gardens Mean?" *Landscape Journal* 24, no. 1 (2006), 95.

4   This Kent drawing is frequently illustrated: see the catalogue of his designs in my *William Kent: Landscape Garden Designer* (London: Zwemmer, 1987), fig. 105.

5   See Michael Bevington, *Stowe: The Garden and the Park* (Stowe: Capability Books, 1994), p. 97.

6   Whately noted (p. 120) that a Greek building might be admitted into a garden if the style was designed to "adorn" the site.

7   See my discussion and illustration of this Grecian Valley in *A World of Gardens* (London: Reaktion Books, 2012), pp. 189–92.

8   Robert Irwin, *Being and Circumstance*, (Larkspur Landing, Calf.: Lapis Press, 1985), p.24.

9   The whole section on water is to be found in *Théorie des jardins, ou l'art des jardins de la Nature* (1803), vol. I, pp. 125–53.

Chapter 5. John Ruskin, Claude Lorrain, Robert Smithson, Christopher Tunnard, Nikolaus Pevsner and Yve-Alain Bois Walked into a Bar . . .

Copyright © 2012 John Dixon Hunt. This article was first published in the *Hopkins Review* 5, no. 1 (2012), 81–94. Reprinted with permission from Johns Hopkins University Press.

The discussion was, alas, not recorded, but the dialogue has been recovered by collating notes left by various parties (included some interesting, but uninvited, interlopers) and from the books that participants and interlopers cited during the debate. They referred to the following writings: Yve-Alain Bois, "A Picturesque Stroll Around *Clara-Clara*," *October* 29 (1984), where he quotes remarks of Smithson and Serra; A. J. Downing, *A Treatise on the Theory and Practice of Landscape Architecture, Adapted to North American* (1841), section 2 on the picturesque; Nikolaus Pevsner, the chapter entitled "Picturesque England" in *The Englishness of English Art* (London: Architectural Press, 1956), and *Visual Planning and the Picturesque*, ed. Matthew Aitchison (Los Angeles: Getty Publications, 2010), with his editor sometimes speaking for him; John Ruskin, "The Lamp of Memory," especially section XII, in *The Seven Lamps of Architecture* (1849) and his first chapter of *Modern Painters* IV (1856) on the picturesque; Robert Smithson, mainly his essays "A Tour of the Monuments of Passaic, New Jersey" and "Frederick Law Olmsted and the Dialectical Landscape," in *The Collected Writings*, ed. Jack Flam (Berkeley: University of California Press, 1996); Christopher Tunnard, *Gardens in the Modern Landscape* (London, second revised edition, 1948, reprt. Philadelphia: University of Pennsylvania Press, 2014); and Anthony Vidler, *Histories of the Immediate Present: Inventing Architectural Modernism* (Cambridge, Mass.: MIT Press, 2008). Other remarks (on Aglionby, Gainsborough. Pope and Addison) seem to have been lifted from John Dixon Hunt, *The Picturesque Garden in Europe* (London: Thames and Hudson, 2003). William Gilpin's dialogue on Stowe is discussed below in Chapter 8.

Chapter 6. Folly in the Garden

1   Barbara Jones in her wonderful *Follies and Grottoes* ([London: Constable, [1953] revised and enlarged edition, 1974) has a more cautious and even-handed approach to defining the folly: see pp. 1–7.

2   The reader is directed to two detailed and very stimulating essays on this rhetorical and literary feature in Geoffrey H. Hartman, *Beyond Formalism: Literary Essays 1958–1970* (New Haven: Yale University Press, 1970), pp. 206–30 and 311–36.

3   On the cult of visiting cultural spots see Nicola J. Watson, *The Literary Tourist: Readers and Places in Romantic and Victorian Britain* (London: Palgrave Macmillan, 2006), notably the chapter on Thomas Gray.

4   Erwin Panofsky, "*Et in Arcadia Ego*: Poussin and the Elegiac Tradition," in

Meaning in the Visual Arts (Garden City, N.Y.: Doubleday Anchor Books, 1955), pp. 295–320. Against which interpretation, read Yves Bonnefoy, "Les berges d'Arcadie," in *Le nuage rouge: Dessin, couleur et lumière* (Paris: Mercure de France, 1990), pp. 277–314.

5   In England, too, Latin meant Roman: a friend of Inigo Jones, who wrote a book on Stonehenge, told him it couldn't be a Roman construction because it had no inscriptions, it was "dumb."

6   I have explored Finlay's modern garden making, and its intersections with neoclassicism, in my *Nature over Again: The Garden Art of Ian Hamilton Finlay* (London: Reaktion Books, 2008). I draw here on a few observations from that book.

7   "Although there is an Apollo Temple, a broken column or two and an avalanche of poetic mottoes and inscriptions, the insistent namedropping of pastoral painters and writers and garden theorists tends to get on one's nerves"; p. 492. The text goes on to complain that the elements in the garden are not "macho."

8   In Augustin Berque et al., *Mouvance: Cinquante mots pour le paysage* (Paris: Éditions de la Villette, 1999), p. 67.

9   This is the recension of Hegel's remark by Roland Barthes, quoted as the motto to my *Greater Perfections: The Practice of Garden Theory*, Penn Studies in Landscape Architecture (Philadelphia: University of Pennsylvania Press; London: Thames & Hudson, 2000).

10   Finlay, personal communication to the author (23 April 1996). In another letter, to Gavin Keeney (but copied to the author), Finlay complained that the National Trust was supposed to "conserve traditions" but had "both mocked and degraded follies and their makers. It is a perfect (sublimlely [*sic*]) imperfect example of secularization."

11   Richard A. Etlin, *The Architecture of Death* (Cambridge, Mass: MIT Press, 1984), p. 146 and figs. 110 and 111.

12   See *Dicovert: Dictionnaire des jardins et paysages,* ed. Philippe Thébaud and Anne Camus (Ris-Organgis: Éditions ARCATURE, 1993), p. 303 (though it is not entirely true to say, as does the entry here on *Folie,* that the word took "un tout autre sense" when it came to refer to some architectural extravagance, for the follies did still "mettre en aleur le parc ou le jardin ou elles étaient édifiés" and thus retained a fossil of original meanings, especially if they were constructed, as many were, of natural materials). See also Michel Conan, *Dictionnaire historique de l'art des jardins* (Paris: Hazan, n.d.), p. 104 ; and Headley and Meulenkamp's National Trust book introduction, p. xxii.

13   Etlin, *The Architecture of Death*, pp. 303–7.

14   On this third site see Roger Wahl, *La Folie Sainte-James* (Neuilly-sur-Seine: Chez l'auteur, 1955), and Gabrielle Joudiou, *La Folie de M. de Sainte-James* (Neuilly-sur-Seine: Éditions Spiralinthe, 2001).

15   *The Correspondence of Alexander Pope,* ed. George Sherburn, 5 vols. (Oxford University Press, 1956), II, 239. There was and still is a seat at Sherborne dedicated to Raleigh.

16   Walpole to Richard Bentley, September 1753, *The Correspondence* , ed. W. S. Lewis and R. S. Brown (New Haven: Yale University Press, 1937), vol. 35, p. 148.

17   I have discussed and illustrated some of these in *The Picturesque Garden in Europe* (London: Thames & Hudson, 2002).

18   Williams Chambers, *A Dissertation on Oriental Gardening* (1772), p. v.

19   Yves Bonnefoy, "Le Désert de Retz et l'expérience du lieu," in *Le nuage rouge,* pp. 368–82, here p. 368.

20   The buttons are illustrated in Gabrielle Joudiou, *La Folie de M.de Sainte-James* (Neuilly-sur-Seine: Éditions Spiralinthe, 2001), pp. 6, 68–69. The same comment was made frequently by Horace Walpole about the many temples in the gardens at Stowe: see his *Correspondence,* vol. 35, p. 75, in a letter to John Chute in August 1777.

21   See Joudiou, *La Folie de M. de Sainte-James,* which is as bewilderingly illustrated and laid out on the page as the original garden itself must have been.

22   Walpole to John Chute, August 1771, cited in Isabel Wakelin Urban Chase, *Horace Walpole: Gardenist* (Princeton: Princeton University Press, 1943), p. 213.

23   The publication consisted of two, substantial brochures published by the Nederlands Architectuurinstituut: a historical survey by Patricia Deiters and Erik de Jong, *Een Paviljoen in Arcadie: Geschiedenis van de Follie,* and the other consisting of folly designs by young Dutch architects.

24   However, another architect, the Greek Aristide Antonas, does imagine his projects as inhabiting actual topographical if not geographical locations: see his *Prospsorika Ktismata / Oral Architecture* (Athens: Patakis Publishing, 2004), with bilingual text. I am grateful to Costis Alexakis for bringing this to my attention.

25   As Tschumi also does with the idea of the garden, examples of which—though he wants to eliminate them—are incorporated but buried below grade and mostly out of sight.

26   I have also explored more extensively the designs of Paolo Bürgi in Switzerland in *Historical Ground: The Role of History in Contemporary Landscape Architecture* (London: Routledge, 2014).

Chapter 7. *Jardins*

1   Denise and Jean-Pierre Le Dantec, *Le roman des jardins de France* (1987), translated by Jessica Levine as *Reading the French Garden: Story and History* (Cambridge, Mass.: MIT Press, 1990). An innovative way of approaching garden history.

2   *St. George Killing the Dragon,* a panel from the 1420s, is in the Art Institute of Chicago, and is illustrated in my *Greater Perfections: The Practice of Garden Theory* (Philadelphia: University of Pennsylvania Press and London: Thames & Hudson, 2000), fig. 17.

3   Illustrated in *A World of Gardens* (London: Reaktion Books, 2012), p. 82 (fig. 56).

4   See Johanna Bauman, "Tradition and Transformation: the Pleasure Garden in Piero de' Crescenzi's *Liber ruralium commodorum,*" *Studies in the History of Gardens and Designed Landscapes* 22 (2012), 99–141.

5   This inquiry by Taegio is studied by Thomas Beck in his translation of *La Villa* (Philadelphia: University of Pennsylvania Press, 2011); see his introduction, pp. 58–69.

6   Turner's painting is illustrated as plate 22 in my *Greater Perfections*.

7   Obrist published his four-page list of different gardens in *Landscape Journal* as "Un Jardin peut en cacher un autre," *Landscape Journal* 21, no. 2 (2002), 15–18.

8   See Patrick Bowe, "The Sacred Grove of Ancient Greece," *Studies in the History of Gardens and Designed Landscapes* 29 (2009), 235–45.

9   See Alfred Runte, *Yosemite: The Embattled Wilderness* (Lincoln,: University of Nebraska Press, 1990), and *Public Nature: Scenery, History and Park Design,* ed. Ethan Carr, Shaun Eyring, and Richard Guy Wilson (Charlottesville: University of Virginia Press, 2013), especially pp. 15–18.

10   Peter Latz, "The Idea of Making Time Visible," *Topos*, 33 (December 2000), p. 85. *An Interview with Garrett Eckbo January 1981* (Watertown, Mass: Hubbard Educational Trust, 1990), p. 12. Bernard Lassus, *The Landscape Approach* (Philadelphia: University of Pennsylvania Press, 1998), p. 72.

11   I have explored this topic explicitly and at length in *The Making of Place: Modern and Contemporary Gardens* (London: Reaktion Books, 2015), where each chapter addresses a specific kind of garden type.

Chapter 8. Between Garden and Landscape

This essay was given as a talk in French at the conference in memory of an old friend and garden historian, Michel Baridon, in May 2010; the title, "Jardin et paysage: Quels liens entre eux?" was taken from one of his last writings and engaged here with that text. Another talk, delivered at Dijon, where Michel was a professor of English, was also given that summer, in English; it is now Chapter 9. The epigraphs for this chapter come, respectively, from Carmontelle, *Jardin de Monceau* (1779), and from Anne Cauquelin, *Petit traité du jardin ordinaire* (Paris: Payot, 2003), p. 10.

1   The French translation is printed *en face* with the English text, using the fourth edition of 1800. All quotations in the text refer to sections of the English publication of Gilpin's *Observations*, published in London in 1800.

2   See Chapter 9 below.

3   My own first visit to Stowe was guided by George Clarke, with copies of the *Dialogue* in our hands.

4   This theme was taken up by the third Earl of Shaftesbury's *Characteristics of Men, Morals, Opinions and Times* and his later *Second Characters or the Language of Forms.* My colleague David Leatherbarrow has discussed this in *Topographical Stories* (Philadelphia: University of Pennsylvania Press, 2004), pp. 131–68.

5   See above in Chapter 4, where this is treated at length.

6   Quote in Sylvia Crowe, *Shaping Tomorrow's Landscape* (Amsterdam: Djaambatab, 1964), p. 18.

7   *Greater Perfections: The Practice of Garden Theory* (Philadelphia: University of Pennsylvania Press, London: Thames and Hudson, 2000), chapter 3. See also above in Chapter 7.

8   David Leatherbarrow's exegesis of Shaftesbury in *Topographical Stories,* chapter 5, is most instructive here. This has always been a tricky text to adjudicate. So a

recent article by Suzannah Fleming, "The 'Convenience of Husbandry' in the Adaptation of the 3rd Earl of Shaftesbury's Garden and Park in Dorset," *Garden History* (Summer 2015), pp. 3–32, challenges some of Leatherbarrow's analysis of Shaftesbury's notes. She does so by proposing an alternative layout for the garden and by citing alternative readings of Shaftesbury's language put forward in Douglas Chamber's *Planters of the English Landscape Garden* (1993). The new readings are interesting but, surely, fail to address the central issue—that Shaftesbury argued for a diminuation of formal or shaped plant materials as a garden or landscape moved away from the house. She makes that precise point herself when noting that the engraving portrait of Shaftesbury shows "dramatic mountain scenery" in the background of a "very simple geometric" foreground with a grove beyond it and before the mountains. This analysis of "character" in garden designs is not the same as arguing for Shaftesbury's "celebration of wilderness" as influencing "later landscapes." What is does offer is a way for early eighteenth-century gardens to see themselves as a *terza* or third nature with a conspectus of alternative renderings. In other words, and relevant to my argument in this essay, there is a distinction between a garden and a landscape.

9   The quotations from Shaftesbury's MS are available in Leatherbarrows's *Topographical Stories,* pp. 265–269.

Chapter 9. Ekphrasis

1   The subject is now much written about: see, among others, James Heffernan, *The Museum of Words: The Poetics of Ekphrasis from Homer to Ashbery* (Chicago: University of Chicago Press, 1993); John Hollander, *The Gazer's Spirit: Poems Speaking to Silent Works of Art* (Chicago: University of Chicago Press, 1995); *Pictures into Words: Theoretical and Descriptive Approaches to Ekphrasis*, ed. Valerie Robillard and Els Jongeneel (Amsterdam:VU University Press, 1998): *Interact Poetics: Essays on the Interrelations of the Arts and Media,* ed. U.-B. Lageroth, Hans Lund, and Erik Hedling (Amsterdam: Rodolfi, 1997); and essays by Ruth Webb and Bergmann Loizeaux in the journal *Word & Image* 15 (1999).

2   John Dixon Hunt, "Ekphrasis of Gardens," *Interfaces: Image Text Langage* 5 (1994), pp. 61–74.

3   *Art History* 33, no. 1 (2010), pp. 10–27.

4   Michel Beaujour, "Some Paradoxes of Description," *Yale French Studies*, 61 (1981), pp. 27–59.

5   In my *William Kent: Landscape Garden Architect: An Assessment and Catalogue Raisonné* (London: Philip Wilson, 1987); "Pope, Kent and 'Palladian' Gardening," in *The Enduring Legacy: Alexander Pope Tercentenary Essays*, ed. Pat Rogers and G. S. Rousseau (Cambridge: Cambridge University Press, 1988); "Verbal Versus Visual Meanings in Garden History: The Case of Rousham," in *Garden History: Issues, Approaches, Methods*, Dumbarton Oaks Colloquium on the History of Landscape Architecture, XIII (Washington, D.C.: Dumbarton Oaks, 1992); and "William Kent as Landscape Architect," catalogue of the Kent Exhibition at the New York Bard

Graduate Centre and the Victoria and Albert Museum in 2013 (New Haven, Conn.: Yale University Press).

6   Actually one has been required to pay for one's entrance and take a ticket from a machine in the stables before visiting.

7   If we compare it with many of the poems selected for my *Oxford Book of Gardens* (1993), we find specific gardens (both nominal or actual, as John Hollander's ekphrastic vocabulary terms them [see above]) are enhanced by assumptions about the art of garden making and using.

8   I am using here David Coffin, "The Elysian Fields of Rousham," in *Magnificent Buildings, Splendid Gardens,* ed. Vanessa Bezemer Sellers (Princeton: Princeton University Press, 2008), pp. 218–31; the pamphlet entitled "Rousham," *New Arcadians' Journal* 19 (1985), which includes (i) the 1750 letter by John Macclary, (ii) an essay by Simon Pugh, and (iii) Patrick Eyres's "iconographic speculation" on "Garden of Apollo and Venus"; and also my own essay in the Dumbarton Oaks volume, *Garden History*, cited in note 5.

9   See Coffin, "The Elysian Fields of Rousham." Yet why the Gothick and northern style should be imposed upon classical items—a Roman "triumphal" arch and a *Temple* of the Mill—are never acknowledged; indeed, this mixture of classical and Gothick is apparent everywhere throughout Rousham and not just to the "north"—crenelations on the façade of the Jacobean house take the form of the Palladian screen on San Giorgio Maggiore in Venice.

10   John Macclary, "A Description of Rousham," transcribed and edited by Mavis Batey, in "The Way to View Rousham by Kent's Gardener," *Garden History* 11 (1983), pp. 125–32, where the editor sees Macclary's route as one intended by Kent himself.

11   See, for instance, James G. Turner, "The Sexual Politics of Landscape: Images of Venus in Eighteenth-Century English Poetry and Gardening," *Studies in Eighteenth-Century Culture* 11 (1982), pp. 343–66, and Coffin's "Venus in the Eighteenth-Century English Garden," in *Magnificent Buildings, Splendid Gardens*, ed. Sellers, pp. 232–49.

12   In my "Emblem and Expression in the Eighteenth-Century Landscape Garden," in *Gardens and the Picturesque: Studies in the History of Landscape Architecture* (Cambridge, Mass.: MIT Press, 1992), p. 86.

13   *The History of the Modern Taste in Gardening* (New York: Ursus Press, 1995), pp. 53–54.

14   This is obviously not a problem only with garden descriptions, as many iconographical accounts may manipulate their materials to argue a particular point

15   Coffin writes that the sculptures on the garden façade of the house were put there by Kent "since one might expect these statues to relate to the iconography of the garden" ("The Elysian Fields of Rousham," p. 226). But even he confesses to "confusing evidence."

16   Coffin, "The Elysian Fields of Rousham," p. 223. But what does "here" actually mean? That something in the Cold Bath does suggest such a meaning? But it is the steward's letter, in the sentences that follow, which does the suggesting in 1750. And

the slippage of the sentence in Coffin from suggestion to acceptance is, at the very least, disarming.

17   Batey, "The Way to View Rousham by Kent's Gardener," 129.

18   Coffin, "The Elysian Fields of Rousham," pp. 224 and 227–28.

19   Batey, "The Way to View Rousham by Kent's Gardener," pp. 128–129, 131.

20   Mitchell's essay "Beyond Comparison: Picture, Text, and Method" appeared in *Interfaces* 5 (1994), pp. 13–38.

21   W. J. T. Mitchell, *Iconology: Image, Text, Ideology* (Chicago: University of Chicago Press, 1986), pp. 43 and 44 (for the following remark). See also his *Picture Theory* (Chicago: University of Chicago Press, 1994), specifically the chapter "Ekphrasis and the Other" (pp. 151–81).

Chapter 10. Preservation in the Sphere of the Mind

1   *Civilization and Its Discontents,* trans. James Strachey (New York: Norton, 1961), p. 16.

2   A version of that talk was then used for this essay (now slightly adjusted), published in the 2005 *Prospectus* for the Graduate Program in Historic Preservation at the University of Pennsylvania.

3   *Cinégram folie, Le Parc de la Villette* (Princeton, N.J.: Princeton Architectural Press, 1987), pp. VIII and I, respectively.

4   *A Dialogue Upon the Gardens at Stow*, Augustan Reprint Society 176 (1976) with introduction by John Dixon Hunt. All in-text references are to this text.

5   *Settings and Stray Paths: Writings on Landscapes and Gardens* (London: Routledge, 2005), p. 128.

6   I discuss this cluster of designs in both *Historical Ground: The Role of History in Contemporary Landscape Architecture* (London: Routledge, 2014) and again in *The Making of Place*, forthcoming (London: Reaktion Books, 2015).

7   *John Constable's Correspondence,* ed. R. B. Beckett (Ipswich: Suffolk Records Society,1968), pp. 77–78.

Chapter 11. ARCH

1   In *Fleur de l'Air: A Garden in Provence by Ian Hamilton Finlay,* ed. Pia Maria Simig (Dunsyre: Wild Hawthorne Press, 2004), note on plates 68, 69, and 70.

2   A first, brief version of this essay was published as "Bridges, Friendship and the Picturesque Garden," in *Wege zum Garten: Gewidmet Michael Seiler zum 65.Geburtsag* (Potsdam: Koehler & Amelang, 2004), pp. 21–25.

3   I illustrate this engraving, where the shadow shows clearly, in *Garden and Grove* (London: Dent, 1986), fig. 75.

4   David R. Marshall, "Gardens and the Death of Art: Robert Irwin's *Getty Garden,*" *Studies in the History of Gardens and Designed Landscapes,* 24 (2004), 215–28, here p. 221. See also Lawrence Weschler, *Robert Irwin Getty Garden* (Los Angeles, 2002).

5   Marshall, "Gardens and the Death of Art," p. 220.

6 I provide a twentieth-century facsimile of these eighteen drawings in *The Picturesque Garden in Europe* (London: Thames and Hudson, 2003), pp. 168–69.

7 Watelet's *Essay on Gardens* was translated and edited by Samuel Danon, with introduction by Joseph Disponzio (Philadelphia: University of Pennsylvania Press, 2003). Page references for quotations in my text are to this edition.

8 See above in Chapter 8.

9 See Terry Friedman, *James Gibbs* (New Haven: Yale University Press, 1984), p. 182.

10 John Ruskin, *Modern Painters,* vol. 3, chap. 12 (1856). I have also consulted the brief explanation of the term in the *Princeton Encyclopedia of Poetry and Poetics,* ed. Alex Preminger (1974 edition).

11 Ruskin's discussion of "The Pathetic Fallacy" is chapter 12 in the third volume of *Modern Painters.*

12 *The Architecture of Humanism: A Study in the History of Taste* (New York: W. W. Norton, 1969), to which edition in-text page numbers refer.

13 I owe this reference and my following up of its suggestion to Gideon Shapiro, who quoted it in a paper he wrote for me. I returned to Scott, unread now for thirty years, and what follows in my text draws in part upon that rereading.

14 See above in Chapter 2.

15 On empathy see: Juliet Koss, "On the Limits of Empathy," *Art Bulletin* 88 (2006), 139–57; Nicolas Le Camus de Mézières, *The Genius of Architecture, or, The Analogy of Art with Our Sensations* (Los Angeles: Getty Publications, 1992); *Empathy, Form and Space: Problems in German Aesthetics 1873–1893,* ed. Harry Francis Mallgrave et al. (Los Angeles: Getty Center, 1994).

16 See Chapter 3. But this raises, I think, the larger question of how empathy or emotion got into the garden (and no doubt into architecture), and moreover how we in our turn get it out of them or understand its potency, or, if you like (if you are a positivist), its fraudulence. (Parenthetically, this topic has a considerable resonance in China: see Peter Blundell Jones and Xeumei Li, "What Can a Bridge Be? The Wind and Rain Bridges of the Dong," *Journal of Architecture* 13, no. 5 [2008], 565–84, with references in particular to the connection of bridges with *feng-shui.*)

17 It is *only* apt in Provence if we accept that the bridge is at the end of the journey through the garden—though presumably we have to climb back up the hillside—or that this garden was created at the very end of Finlay's life (though, again, we know this only with hindsight).

18 Martin Heidegger, *Poetry, Language, Thought,* trans. Albert Hofstadter (New York: Harper & Row, 1977, 1971), p. 152. My in-text page references are to this edition.

19 This, as my anonymous reader reminds me, is similar to Wallace Stevens's poem, "A Jar upon the Hill," where the insertion of the jar transforms how we see the hillside.

20 See also Richard Anderson, "Tired of Meaning," *Log* 7 (Winter–Spring 2006), 11–13.

21 Peter Eisenmann, quoted in Anderson, ibid., p. 11.

22 See Koss, "On the Limits of Empathy," p. 139.

Index

Index

Index

Index